SWIFT

FROM THE COCKPIT, No 14

NIGEL WALPOLE

PUBLICATIONS

Contents

INTRODUCTION *Group Captain Nigel Walpole* OBE BA 4

TRIALS AND TRIBULATIONS *Group Captain Nigel Walpole* OBE BA 8

Record Breakers *Group Captain Nigel Walpole* OBE BA 26

DIFFICULTIES (CONTD.) *Group Captain Nigel Walpole* OBE BA 28

Pride and Enthusiasm *Group Captain G. J. ('Twinkle') Storey* 32

We Lucky Few *Flight Lieutenant Richard Carrey* 34

Mixed Feelings *Squadron Leader Jock Byrne* MBE QCVSA 38

Waiting for Thicker Air *Air Vice-Marshal Peter Collins* CB AFC BA 40

'Stop That!' *Squadron Leader Roy Rimington* 42

RENAISSANCE *Group Captain Nigel Walpole* OBE BA 44

COURTESY BRIAN LUFFINGHAM

FROM THE COCKPIT *Group Captain Nigel Walpole* OBE BA 52
'Get Swept!' *Flight Lieutenant Brian Luffingham* 74
No Instant Response *Squadron Leader Bob Broad* 78
Sixth Sense *Squadron Leader Phil Crawshaw* MBE 80
Close to the Deck *Group Captain B. W. ('Danny') Lavender* OBE AFC 82
The Well-Built Swift *Air Commodore Pat King* CBE 85
Fun to Fly *Group Captain John Turner* 87
TESTING FOR THE FUTURE *Group Captain Nigel Walpole* OBE BA 88
SQUADRONS AND COLOURS 94
Flown by the Author 100
GONE BUT NOT FORGOTTEN *Group Captain Nigel Walpole* OBE BA 102

Below: Four Swift F.R.5s from the author's squadron—No 79—led by (background) Flight Lieutenant Paul Worthington in XD925 and with Flying Officer Brian Luffingham in XD952/'B', Flight Lieutenant Lou Cockerill in XD953/'F' and Flying Officer Ian Waller in XD913 (foreground) in accompaniment.

INTRODUCTION

Group Captain Nigel Walpole OBE BA

IN the early 1950s, events in Berlin, the conflict in Korea and the prospect of Armageddon as the Cold War developed provided a wake-up call for a British Government that had allowed its once mighty military machine to wind down in the wake of victory in World War II. In particular, the air war in the sky over Korea underlined the vital need for a new breed of air defence fighters to replace the RAF's obsolescent Meteors, Vampires and Venoms, and to match the American F-86 Sabres and Russian MiG-15s.

The two great British aircraft companies, Vickers-Armstrong Supermarine and Hawker, their heritage already enshrined in aviation history, had foreseen the need for such a jet fighter and were preparing to do battle for the contract they anticipated. In 1944, the Air Ministry and Ministry of Supply had asked Supermarine to evaluate two prototypes of a jet aircraft the company had under construction, which would incorporate the laminar-flow wings then undergoing trials on its piston-engined Spiteful. When this aircraft emerged as the Attacker, its performance was found to be little better than that of the Meteor and Vampire, and it was rejected by the RAF. The Attacker did, however, see service with the Royal Navy until replaced by the Hawker Sea Hawk.

Supermarine's chief designer, Joe Smith, then persuaded the Air Ministry that swept flying surfaces could be mounted on a suitably modified Attacker fuselage, and in so doing secured a contract based on Air Ministry Specification E.41/46, to evaluate two experimental aircraft, designated Type 510; they were given the serial numbers VV106 and VV109. At the same time, Hawker were pursuing a similar path with a swept-wing version of its P.1040, to be known as the P.1052, they too earning a contract to produce a pair of aircraft, numbered VX272 and VX279, to meet the Ministry's Specification E.38/46. The

COURTESY PHILIP JARRETT

Left: Supermarine's 'jet machine of the Spiteful type'—the wings were in essence those of this ultimate Spitfire derivative—was not adopted by the Royal Air Force although it was developed into the Attacker, which became the first Royal Navy jet fighter to enter squadron service. Below: The Attacker prototype, the Supermarine 392, did, however, form the basis for the company's Type 510, which in turn spawned the Type 535 and so the Swift. VV106 was the first of a pair of Type 510s. Leaving aside the swept flying surfaces, the resemblance to the Type 392 is unmistakable.

aircraft from both companies would be powered by Rolls-Royce Nene 2 turbojet engines producing 5,000 pounds of thrust. It was now 1947, and by the end of that year the F-86 and the MiG-15 were already flying, yet still the British programme to produce an equivalent fighter lacked impetus. However, the competition between the two companies was now on, and although these aircraft were deemed to be solely 'experimental', there was, clearly, every hope that each could be developed into

COURTESY PHILIP JARRETT

COURTESY PHILIP JARRETT

Above, right and below: As in most areas of technical achievement, progress involves proceeding from the known to the unknown, and, like Supermarine's, Hawker's contender for the Meteor replacement aircraft owed its existence to a number of earlier designs that were, stage by stage, built, exhaustively tested and improved. The first production jet fighter from the Kingston-upon-Thames premises was the straight-winged Sea Hawk, the prototype for which was the P.1040 (above). A swept-wing development was the P.1052 (right), and the immediate prototype for the aircraft which would be taken into service by the RAF as the Hunter was the P.1067 (below). Again, the lineage is very obvious.

COURTESY BRIAN LOWE

BAE SYSTEMS

COURTESY PHILIP JARRETT

Right: The Supermarine Type 510 VV106 in flight; it was the first British swept-wing jet aircraft to take to the air, a distinction that it achieved on 29 December 1948. The pilot, Mike Lithgow, eventually took the aircraft to a speed of 0.93M (Mach 0.93). It was a generally successful aircraft, imparted invaluable data for the design team and promised well for the series production of a front-line fighter aircraft.
Below: VV106 on display at the Farnborough Air Show in September 1949, where it was demonstrated with aplomb by Lithgow and generally impressed. The somewhat anachronistic tailwheel undercarriage was inherited directly from the Type 392.

a state-of-the-art fighter interceptor. The Hawker P.1052 flew first in November 1948 and the Supermarine 510 one month later. They were breaking new ground, with very little known at the time about the efficacy of swept wings in high subsonic, transonic and supersonic flight, and the learning curve was steep. It was, therefore, understandable that when the associated Operational Requirement No 228 (Issue 3) emerged in 1951, specifications as to manœuvre boundaries and performance at these speeds and at high level were left deliberately imprecise.

As research into the two aircraft progressed, mainly at the Aeroplane and Armament Experimental Establishment (A&AEE) at Boscombe Down, so speculation grew as to which variant should be the RAF's primary day fighter for the 1950s, which would offer the best performance and which could reach the flight line first. It would be some time before a conclusive, objective comparison could be made between the two aircraft types, but early indications were that the 510 would lose out to the P.1052 in performance although it might win the race to the front line. These assumptions led to protracted discussions about whether the embryo Supermarine fighter should act as a 'stopgap' or an 'interim' fighter, as an insurance against the failure of the Hawker aircraft, or whether there could be complementary rôles for the two aircraft. In 1953, a compromise was reached to cover all contingencies: the primary contract went to Hawker for what would become the Hunter and another was issued to Supermarine for 150 Swifts. This in no way deterred Supermarine, and both companies continued their unstinting efforts to make a success of their respective aircraft.

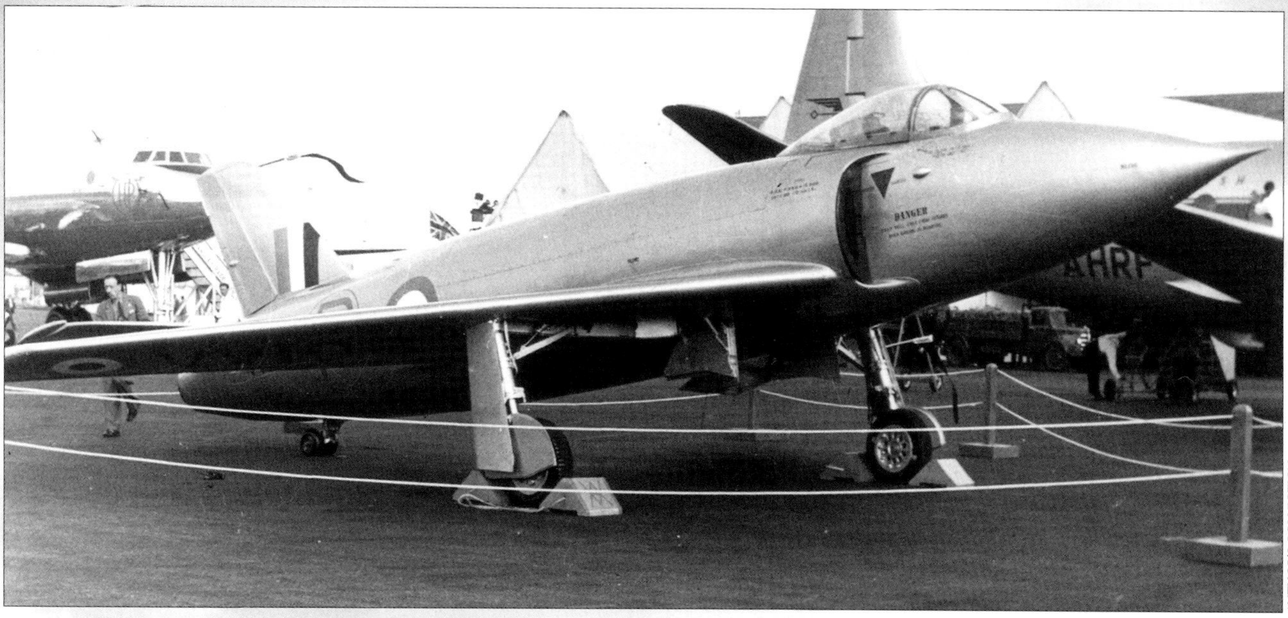

AUTHOR'S COLLECTION

TRIALS AND TRIBULATIONS

Group Captain Nigel Walpole OBE BA

THE first of Supermarine's two experimental aircraft, VV106, retained the Attacker's bulbous fuselage to house the centrifugal-flow Nene engine, and a tailwheel configuration, but it spawned swept wings and tailplane. The aircraft was built at the company's headquarters, Hursley Park, and made its maiden flight from Boscombe Down on 29 December 1949 before going to Supermarine's airfield at Chilbolton for initial flight tests. It then returned to Boscombe Down for more intensive trials.

As with any new venture into uncharted waters, there were bound to be problems. In particular, VV106 encountered engine vibration and directional instability at low power settings, found to be caused by engine air intake turbulence, which called for modifications to the forward engine mountings and boundary layer bleeds above and below the intakes. The swept flying surfaces produced few of the adverse effects expected, although the aircraft tended to 'self-tighten' in the turn, elevator forces became heavy during large displacements, the absence of an air brake was regretted and cross-wind landings could be tricky. In 1950, the Royal Aircraft Establishment (RAE) at Farnborough used the aircraft to carry out extensive research into this configuration during high-subsonic and low-speed flight. This revealed some undesirable handling tendencies, typically a very high sink rate at the stall and a reluctance for the aircraft to recover even with the stick fully forward and full power applied. While at RAE, the aircraft was fitted with Rocket-Assisted Take-Off Gear (RATOG) and an arrester hook, to practise deck take-offs and landings there before completing successful deck operations at sea on board HMS *Illustrious* in November 1950. On the last sortie, the aircraft did have a slight *contretemps* with the carrier's port gun turret, following an asymmetric rocket ignition, but it was landed safely, thanks to the skill

Below: VV106, flaps deployed in the landing configuration. The aircraft was employed in trials for many years and has been preserved: it is now in the custody of the Fleet Air Arm Museum at RNAS Yeovilton.

AUTHOR'S COLLECTION

Right: A historic 'first', 8 November 1950: VV106, piloted by Lieutenant Jock Elliot, becomes the first swept-wing aeroplane to land on board—and, later that day, take off from—an aircraft carrier. The venue is HMS *Illustrious*. It can be seen that the aircraft is fitted with RATOG. Below: VV106 underwent a number of modifications as testing progressed; for example, it originally had a rounded nose, as here.

COURTESY PHILIP JARRETT

of the pilot, Lieutenant-Commander Doug Parker, and the strength of the aircraft. Throughout this period, the aircraft also suffered several flame-outs, but again its robust construction enabled it to survive two wheels-up landings—after each of which it was soon back in the air. VV106 had served well in its primary rôle as a test vehicle for swept wings, providing data on potential control problems at the extremes of its speed range. From the start of its life it had flown regularly at speeds of 0.9M and above

BAE SYSTEMS

AUTHOR'S COLLECTION

and had achieved 550 knots in level flight and 585 knots in a shallow dive; it had, moreover, proved a useful 'guinea pig' for a number of enterprising innovations.

The second experimental 510, VV119, flew for the first time at Boscombe Down on 27 March 1950,

Above and below: The second Type 510, VV119, was, in its first incarnation, broadly identical to VV106, but, having made a small number of flights from 27 March 1950, it was extensively redesigned, emerging that summer as the Type 535. Amongst the many changes were the fitting of a tricycle undercarriage (although the tailwheel assembly was retained), a broader rear fuselage (to accommodate a reheated Nene engine), the introduction of a fin fillet, intakes of increased size, a revised wing planform, a framed cockpit canopy, increased fuel capacity and a longer, reshaped nose.

initially in the same configuration as VV106 but incorporating the changes found necessary in that aircraft. It then underwent a major modification programme to include a larger wing with greater sweepback, wing fences, a cranked trailing edge and parallel flaps. Although the twin tail wheels were retained, a tricycle undercarriage was introduced in an extended nose, thereby alleviating the jet-wash problem and improving the aircraft's manœuvrability on the ground, *inter alia* distinguishing it clearly from its predecessor. Presaging the future, provision was made for four wing-mounted guns, although these were never fitted. A simple two-stage reheat was also fitted to the aircraft's Nene Mk 3 engine, until the extra weight was found to cancel out the advantage of the extra thrust provided and it was removed. Likewise, when an experimental air brake on the upper wing caused severe buffeting, it, too, was removed, the first 35 degrees of the huge flaps then being brought into use for that purpose. (Perhaps surprisingly, this proved very effective, requiring little or no trim change when the air brake was operated below Mach 0.94M.) In 1951, despite this very heavy workload and intensive trials, VV119 took time out to star as 'Prometheus' in David Lean's film *The Sound Barrier*, some of the footage for which was taken during test flights.

VV119 joined VV109 in retirement in 1955, having done enough to reassure the Establishment that it had been the right decision to persist with the aircraft, and in November 1950, the Ministry awarded Supermarine a formal contract for two prototypes and 100 fighters. These aircraft would be based on VV119 but have the slimmer Avon RA.7 engine, which increased power and at the same time left space in the capacious fuselage for additional fuel. An improved reheat system would be added and yet more fuel made available from a 220-gallon ventral drop tank. The flight controls were to be fully powered, though have a back-up manual reversion system, while a variable-incidence tailplane would give improved manœuvrability; a cartridge starter was incorporated and the wing-mounted 20mm guns were replaced by four 30mm Aden cannon in the nose.

Operational Requirement 228 (Issue 3), which followed in January 1951, required the aircraft to be able to climb to 45,000 feet in six minutes, hold

AUTHOR'S COLLECTION

0.95M at that height and reach a maximum altitude of 50,000 feet, where it was to have 'the best possible manœuvrability'. This was to be a high-level fighter. RAE studies suggested, however, that these ambitious objectives would be hard to achieve with the aircraft's present wing form—and so it would prove. Above all, however, there was a need to get the Hunter and the Swift into service without unnecessary delay, and further improvements (other than safety imperatives), such as additional weapons fits, would have to wait. It was now envisaged that 150 Swifts could start to be delivered in 1952, followed by 650 Hunters from 1953.

Mike Lithgow got airborne in the first pre-production Swift prototype, WJ960, on 1 August 1951, and immediately proclaimed it to be a vast improvement in performance over the experimental VV119, on which it had been modelled. On 3 August, a ruptured fuel line in this aircraft caused him to carry out a highly skilful flame-out landing at Chilbolton, and four weeks later test pilot David Morgan followed suit, this time landing the aircraft in open country at Charity Down Farm. Such was the strength of the aircraft that it was flying again three months later, for David to break the air speed record between London and Brussels in June 1952. The aircraft completed its schedule of development flying a year later, to end its useful employment as an engine test-bed.

It was David Morgan who took the second pre-production prototype, WJ965, the aircraft which was said to be the first true Swift, on its inaugural flight from Boscombe Down on 18 July 1952. This was indeed more like the fighter to be, with its new cockpit, improved controls, a larger fin, more fuel and the pitot head moved from the nose to the starboard wing tip. In an attempt to save weight, a thinner, lighter skin covered the outer mainplanes, the worrying flutter which resulted quickly alleviated by replacing the spring tabs with geared tabs. This was the aircraft in which, in February 1954, David Morgan exceeded the speed of sound, much to the delight of the aircraft makers at Chilbolton who witnessed the event. In fact, the aircraft flew itself through the sound barrier in the dive, its recovery possible only by throttling back and waiting until it reached denser air below, when the pilot was able to effect a controlled recovery. This mattered little to

COURTESY PHILIP JARRETT

Left and below: The Type 535 was ordered into production as the Type 541, or Swift, and WJ960 was the first of a pair of pre-production aircraft. It first flew on 1 August 1951 and was generally similar to the 535 except that was equipped with a Roll-Royce Avon engine of 7,500 pounds of thrust—fifty per cent more than that of the Nene. The tailwheel assembly was still in evidence, as can be seen in the photograph at left.

COURTESY PHILIP JARRETT

COURTESY PHILIP JARRETT

Left: WJ960 airborne; the new wing shape—of broader chord in its inboard section than that of the original Type 510—may be compared with that in the photograph on page 8.

Below: A glimpse into Supermarine's workshop at Hursley Park, autumn 1952, with the second pre-production Swift, WK965 (foreground), in company with VV119 and the first two production Swifts. WK965's rear fuselage and tailplane have been fitted with wool tufts in connection with investigations into airflow patterns. The photograph clearly shows the considerable forward extension to the main intakes in production aircraft as compared with those of VV119. Notice too, that whereas the pre-production aircraft retain their natural metal surfaces, WK194 and WK195 have been sprayed in High-Speed Silver, the standard RAF day fighter finish of the early 1950s.

AUTHOR'S COLLECTION

the test pilots, but it would have been unacceptable in RAF service, so VI tails were fitted to the operational aircraft to enable control to be maintained throughout transonic flight. Modifications were then made to strengthen the outer wings, replace the flaps to improve their use as air brakes and add aileron power units and a central power control, all of which brought WJ965 very close to the standard of early production models.

The first pre-production Swift, WK194, flew in August 1952, powered by an Avon RA.7 engine and equipped with two 30mm Aden cannon. The firm's test pilots were now joined by service pilots from A&AEE and RAE, one of whom, Chris Clark, reported residual pre-stall instability, tightening in turns, severe wing drop at the stall and intense aileron buzz at high IAS. Supermarine claimed to have remedies for all these deficiencies in hand, but sadly they could not be completed before a US Offshore Procurement team arrived at Chilbolton to

Above: WJ965 at the 1952 Farnborough Show. The aircraft was temporarily grounded following the disintegration of the D.H.110 prototype fighter at the event and the tragic death of De Havilland test pilot John Derry.
Below: WK194, one of the early production Mk 1s but still not quite the definitive service aircraft
Right: WJ965 again, here in plan form and modified to Mk 1 delivery standard. The nose pitot probe has been shifted to the starboard wing and chordwise fences have been added in an attempt to cure pitch-up, exacerbated by the introduction of inboard wing leading-edge extensions in the Swift Mk 2—with highly unfortunate results.

COURTESY TONY BUTTLER

COURTESY TONY BUTLER

Above: Swift pre-production and production Mk 1s under inspection at Hursley Park, showing the evolution in the aircraft's fin shape. These were the only Swifts built as this facility; the rest would be assembled at South Marston.

evaluate the Swift and Hunter as replacement fighters for NATO's European Allies. The team was reported to have been 'favourably impressed' by the Hunter but not by the Swift, if only because of its lack of control at high Mach numbers, its wing drop and its instability at low IAS.

At this point, the Supermarine development programme was disrupted by a decision to have all the available Swifts take part in the Coronation Fly Past at RAF Odiham on 15 July 1953. So it was that six of the aircraft took to the air on the day, only to have Mike Lithgow suffer the much feared flame-out immediately after overflying Odiham, although he was able to make another copy-book 'dead-stick' landing at Chilbolton. Shortly thereafter, the flame-outs which had been plaguing the fleet became very much less frequent when a defect was discovered in a compressor blade's fir-tree root fixture, attributed to an unauthorised redesign by a sub-contractor.

With the Russian MiG-17 now the threat, pressure was increasing to get the Swift and the Hunter into front-line service, but there was still much for A&AEE to do before they could issue the necessary

COURTESY PHILIP JARRETT

Above: Swift fuselages and, far left, Attackers in production at Supermarine's South Marston plant.
Below: Brand new Swift F.1s await delivery to the Royal Air Force at South Marston, February 1954. The Mk 1's nose housed a ranging radar—primitive equipment by today's standards—and, offset to port, a G.45 cine gun camera (the reason for the shallow 'trough'). The two Aden cannon were accommodated in the fuselage belly, adjacent to the wing root leading edge.

clearances. Every hope was placed in a fully instrumented WJ965 sent to Boscombe Down for intensive trials in November 1953, until it crashed there a few days after arriving, killing the pilot, Squadron Leader Ned Lewis. However, the formal trials were resumed at the beginning of 1955, using the first two production Swift F.1s, WK201 and WK202, with A&AEE ordered to produce the earliest possible Controller Aircraft (CA) release for the Swift, based solely on 'the bare essentials to enable the aircraft to be flown safely for pilot familiarisation'. This was easier said than done, but under great pressure from London, and with some apprehension among the test pilots, a 'Restricted Release'—to become known sardonically on the flight line as the 'Fast Taxying Release'—was issued on 12 February 1954, clearing the aircraft to fly up to 500 knots below 5,000 feet,

COURTESY PHILIP JARRETT

COURTESY PHILIP JARRETT

Left: Wing Commander H. Bird-Wilson DSO DFC AFC poses with Swift Mk 1 WK212. The photograph shows the retractable foot holds for aircrew entry and the geometry of the boundary layer air bleed louvres adjacent to the main intake; notice also the sizeable wing fences fitted to production aircraft.
Below: Another view of production Swift F.1s at South Marston, ready for transfer to the RAF.
Right, upper: WK247, the first of the twenty-five Swift Mk 3s to be built. In a further effort to cure handling problems, vortex generators were fitted to the tailplane—though only, as can be seen, to the starboard unit. Like the Mk 2s, the Swift F.3s were completed in the newly introduced disruptive grey/green camouflage scheme, and four Aden cannon were carried.
Right, lower: Swift Mk 3s lined up at South Marston and awaiting delivery. In the event, they would not be taken into service.

then to 0.9M below 25,000 feet, with spinning prohibited. Thus it was that, with much publicity, the first Swift F.1s and F.2s began to arrive at Waterbeach on 20 February 1954 for front-line pilots to add their opinions on the aircraft. Many more trials and tribulations ahead lay for this evolutionary aircraft before anyone could be satisfied that it would make a credible high-level fighter.

A&AEE still had much work to do, as had the all-important Air Fighting Development Squadron (AFDS), whose very critical operational pilots would evaluate the Swift's potential for its intended purpose. The first direct indications AFDS had of the difficulties which beset the Swift came when its commander, Wing Commander 'Birdie' Bird-Wilson, a much-respected World War II fighter pilot, flew a production F.1 at Chilbolton on 3 October 1953. In order to simulate the type of regime that might be encountered in combat, he climbed at once to 42,000 feet and initiated a tight turn at a high angle of attack, until the speed bled off to 160 knots—at which point the engine flamed out. He was able to relight the engine, but he repeated this sequence twice during the following day and with the

COURTESY PHILIP JARRETT

BAE SYSTEMS

COURTESY PHILIP JARRETT

COURTESY PHILIP JARRETT

same results, thus convincing him that Supermarine had much more work to do in this area. The company claimed that these results of his actions were inevitable with the Avon RA.7 engine, when subjected to these conditions, and suggested (perhaps unwisely) that they did not reflect the imperatives of contemporary combat. 'Birdie' thought differently.

At Boscombe Down, A&AEE remained very concerned over a tendency for the aircraft to pitch up at high Mach numbers and low 'g' forces, diminishing elevator control above 0.9M, wing drop from 0.92 to 0.94, and a nose-down change of trim when operating the air brake above 0.94M. These problems, together with a marked tendency for the Avon engine to surge at high altitude in all the expected operating regimes, were exacerbated when it came to fitting the four Aden cannon and associated ammunition containers in leading edge extensions at the wing roots of the F.2, a 'vicious' pitch-up now occurring above 0.85M. The solution was to move the centre of gravity forward by fitting ballast in the nose—but this extra weight then degraded performance. Despite all the efforts of Supermarine and A&AEE to eradicate these faults, in sometimes less than wholly amicable relationships, the F.2 proved no better, overall, than the F.1 as a fighting machine, and could only be released for 'non-operational' flying within the CA constraints of its predecessor.

Then came the F.3, with a reheated Avon 108, improved power controls and modifications found

COURTESY PHILIP JARRETT

Opposite page: Swift Mk 3s await a decision as to their future at the manufacturer's plant. WK247 is nearest.
Above and below: WK247 was the first production F.3 and was exhibited with a weapons load comprising a single 1,000-pound bomb beneath the starboard wing and a clutch of rocket projectiles beneath the port.

necessary during the trials on the earlier variants. In particular, the mainplane now had 'saw-tooth' leading edges, which allowed pitch-up to be controlled and improved the Swift's handling characteristics generally, particularly its manœuvrability at high level and in the approach and landing configuration. Performance in reheat was now very impressive (if very demanding in terms of fuel consumption), and the engine still had a tendency to surge and flame-out, often with some reluctance to relight. While a revised CA Release was offered, it continued to allow non-operational flying only, albeit now unrestricted, but the clearance still fell far short of that required for an operational fighter and was rejected, and none of the 25 F.3s built reached the front line.

All hope for the fighter now rested on the F.4, the first prototype of which (WK198), a modified F.1 and a future record-breaker, made its maiden flight on 3 May 1953, but A&AEE did not begin its formal evaluation of the first pre-production F.4 (WK272) until the end of 1954. This was a markedly different aircraft from its predecessors, with a reheated Avon 114 engine, a VI tail, leading-edge extensions (to reduce the buffeting encountered on the F.3 wing) and a taller fin (to improve directional stability when the ventral fuel tank was fitted). A&AEE now found the aircraft manageable throughout the speed range, with no problems in the transonic zone; the rate of climb was impressive and the reheat could now be engaged reliably below 25,000 feet. Crucially,

COURTESY PHILIP JARRETT

however, with its present wing, the aircraft lacked the necessary manœuvrability above 40,000 feet and could not be expected to prevail in combat against contemporary fighters above 15,000 feet. It therefore remained unacceptable for the rôle intended and none of the four F.4s produced was delivered to the front line.

The AFDS received the first of its F.1s (WK201 and WK202) at West Raynham in February 1954 and its pilots were quick to endorse the findings of A&AEE. Their report to the Air Ministry extolled the virtues of the Swift's starting system, rate of climb to 30,000 feet, rate of roll and braking system, but deplored the poor elevator control at high levels and speeds and during the operation of the air brake. Viewing it also from a combat perspective, they found the tendency for the engine to surge and its compressor stall 'totally unacceptable'. In summary, they thought the aircraft adequate for interceptions at medium levels against the Soviet bombers of the time but that, above 30,000 feet, its radius of turn would render corrections by the pilot more difficult, placing a greater onus on the ground controllers to reach a satisfactory firing solution. These conclusions were supported in practice combat against the more agile Venoms and F-86 Sabres, which simulated the tactics employed by contemporary MiG fighters. Moreover, they found it difficult to maintain optimum positions in battle formation, the poor rearward view from the aircraft requiring wider spacing and adding to their problems in cross-over turns; they likened tactical formation flying in the Swift at 30,000 feet to that in the now obsolescent Venoms and Sabres at 40,000 feet. AFDS therefore recommended that battle

Right and below: The Swift Mk 4, which, it was said, would mark the culmination of all the design revisions and represent the finished article. It didn't—and the concept of the Swift interceptor fighter died with it. WK198 did, however, enjoy a brief moment of glory when it captured the World Air Speed record. The redesigned tailpipe to accommodate reheat is clearly seen in the main illustration.

AD HOC COLLECTION

COURTESY PHILIP JARRETT

COURTESY PHILIP JARRETT

COURTESY TONY BUTTLER

COURTESY PHILIP JARRETT

Opposite page, above and left: A trio of F.1s assigned to the AFDS and formating for a publicity sortie. The portly fuselage, inherited from the Type 510 which was powered by a centrifugal engine and needed the space, was useful when the slimmer axial-flow Avon was introduced as more fuel could be crammed in—but the Swift was still critically short-ranged.
Below: One of the trio, WK205, using half flap, takes off from West Raynham. Notice the extended tailskid; the original twin tailwheel, which served the same function of protecting the lower rear fuselage during take-off and landing, was discontinued on production Swifts.

COURTESY PHILIP JARRETT

Record Breakers *Group Captain Nigel Walpole* OBE BA

The early Swifts deserve proper recognition for their air speed record achievements, recognition more often given to those earned by its close contemporary in the mid-1950s, the Hunter.

David Morgan claimed to have been the first to fly the Swift into the records when he took the pre-production prototype WJ960 from London to Brussels in July 1952, only nine months after the aircraft had so nearly met its end on Charity Down. He covered the distance in 18 minutes at 667mph—and it is believed that this record still stands. Then came Mike Lithgow's record breaking run from London to Paris and back, aboard the prototype F.4, WK198. He set forth on 5 July 1953, beginning the outbound leg in visual contact with the ground at 1,000 feet, but the visibility deteriorated rapidly as he crossed into France. Poor communications then added to his navigation problems and he was said to have been greatly relieved when the Eiffel Tower loomed up ahead after 19 minutes, 5.6 seconds. The return leg was uneventful, and he completed the round trip of 424 miles in a total of 40 minutes, at an average speed of 669.3mph.

WK198 would take the limelight again, but while Neville Duke's record-breaking Hunter WB188, resplendent in its red livery and with its pointed nosecone, continues to gather admirers at the Tangmere Military Aviation Museum, WK198, which took that record from the Hunter, decayed for many years in a scrap metal dealer's yard and only pieces of it now remain. To be sure, the Hunter was the first British aircraft to secure this prestigious accolade from the American F-86D Sabre, flying along the South Coast from RAF Tangmere on 7 September 1953, but Mike Lithgow beat it in WK198 only eighteen days later, on 25 September. On 22 September 1953 Mike flew WK198 from Chilbolton to Idris airfield in Libya, where the hot climate was more conducive to the objective of improving on the Hunter's record speed of 727.6mph. He was supported by Supermarine test pilot Les Colquhoun in an Attacker and a strong team of twelve from the firm, led by Charles Barter, and a group of engine specialists from Rolls-Royce. In its unpretentious garb of light blue, with a black band around the forward fuselage to aid identification, the aircraft was basically a standard F.4 but with the wing fences removed and a special cockpit cooling system that would feed cold air to Mike's air-ventilated flying suit. Colquhoun remembers that there was little preparation for the record attempt itself, which was to be flown over a strip of road in the desert south-east of Tripoli, marked additionally by coloured smoke flares. The route had been surveyed officially by the Ordnance Survey Office and the attempt would be supervised by officials from the Royal Aero Club, according to *Fédération Aéronautique International* rules. They would orbit at either end of the three-kilometre course, clear of

BAE SYSTEMS

Above: One of the many publicity photographs of WJ960.

the Swift's flight path, in an Anson and a Meteor, to ensure that Mike kept to the rules.

At 1430 hours on 25 September Mike began the record attempt, flying at maximum speed in reheat at 100 feet. It soon became clear that all was not well in the cockpit: the ventilated suit failed to deal effectively with temperatures which exceeded those anticipated, a defective fuel gauge gave concern, and a sticking oxygen valve forced the pilot to tear off his mask at the most critical time, thereby causing the aircraft to jink alarmingly and affecting his radio 'patter'. Moreover, heavy turbulence made precise control difficult and probably caused a loss of speed of some 10–15 mph, while making it a challenge to keep the marker flares in sight and to follow the required track precisely. Despite all this, all the four runs called for were completed on that very hot afternoon, the team being credited with a record speed of 737.3mph (later downgraded to 735.7mph). Further attempts to improve on this were abandoned after the ground recording equipment failed, the aircraft had reheat problems and the weather began to fall below acceptable limits, but the team had done enough.

This had been a low-cost, time-sensitive exercise, funded by the firm, which had succeeded. Little had been lost from the trials and development programme, while much had been learned about operations in very hot temperatures, and Supermarine had seized the World Air Speed Record. All this brought tributes from throughout the aviation world, bestowing great credit on Mike Lithgow and all others involved, while enhancing the reputation of British industry.

Above: Few photographs of WK198 in its record-breaking configuration appear to exist, but this distant view of the aircraft in Tunisian skies is one of them.

BAE SYSTEMS

Right: The first production Swift F. Mk 1, WK194.
Below: WK205 is prepared for flying at West Raynham, with refuelling hose and external electrical supply connected and, just above the wing leading edge, the Coffman cartridge starter being reloaded. The groundcrewman forward is perched on the cockpit access step: unusually for an RAF single-seat fighter, the pilot was obliged to enter the cockpit from the starboard side; the wing-tip pitot tube was also on the opposite side to that normally seen.

COURTESY TONY BUTTLER

formation with four Swifts be limited to below 35,000 feet, and pairs of aircraft to below 40,000 feet—which would put the aircraft at a marked disadvantage against it adversaries. As for low-level interceptions, AFDS warned that at speeds in excess of 0.9M the aircraft would have to be handled with great care. Analysing these findings, the Central Fighter Establishment (CFE) concluded that the Swift F.1 had a poor operational ceiling, poor manœuvrability and poor handling at high Mach numbers, with the engine tending to flame out at low IAS and high angles of attack. Moreover, the all-important rearward visibility was bad, as it was in the forward hemisphere at high speeds in heavy rain, particularly when ice and dust gathered between the front screen and armoured glass. In sum, the F.1 could not match other fighters already on the front line and would be barely adequate against bombers up to 30,000 feet. CFE also noted that the West Raynham trials had been carried out without gun sights or the clearance needed to fire the guns—fundamental requirements for combat evaluations. It was clear that very major modifications would be required to remedy these deficiencies but, apart from advocating better elevator control, CFE went no further at this point than to recommend a number of peripheral measures, such as the introduction of a clear-vision canopy, the addition of a mirror, and an improvement to the demisting and de-icing systems. In 1954, AFDS would also evaluate the F.4, a much better aircraft for the job but one it still found unacceptable for the rôle of high-level fighter. However, its report to come on the Swift F.R.5, an aircraft optimised for low level, would tell a different story.

COURTESY PHILIP JARRETT

DIFFICULTIES (CONTD.)

Group Captain Nigel Walpole OBE BA

ARMED with the 'Fast Taxying Release', the first Swift F.1s, led by WK209, began to arrive on No 56 Squadron, RAF Waterbeach, on 20 February 1954. Flying Officer Chris Christie got a bird's eye view of the new aircraft, as he and his leader, piloting Meteors, met and escorted the Swift into the circuit at 'The Beach'. Thus the Swift ushered in a new era of fast-jet flying for the RAF, one very different from that of strictly subsonic flying with the first generation of British jet aircraft, the Meteors and Vampires—but, sadly, this evolutionary aircraft would never fulfil its promise as an air defence fighter.

After the relative simplicity of the Meteor cockpit, the front-line pilots of No 56 Squadron now had to get used to a cockpit full of unfamiliar controls and a frightening array of 'dolls' eyes' to add to the well-proven warning lights. These innovative dolls' eyes tended to chatter away, turning white to signal that some action had taken place or needed to be taken, and sometimes, rather disconcertingly, they continued to do so throughout a flight. The warning lights that indicated whether elevator and aileron power controls were fully engaged or not were particularly important: a false lock in the air spelt serious trouble, and the difference between the highly responsive power control and heavy manual (that is, reversionary) control of the aircraft was very marked. There being no dual-control Swift nor dynamic flight simulator, aircrew had to depend on systems diagrams, Pilot's Notes and a cockpit mock-up which incorporated lights and dolls' eyes operated from an instructor's console. Pilots new to the Swift then spent time in the actual cockpit, to familiarise themselves further with the controls and displays, before their first flight. For many, this was their first taste of the very impressive acceleration and high speeds in all operations carried out by this new breed of fast jet, and, for most, this was also their first acquaintance with an axial-flow jet engine, as opposed to the centrifugal-flow powerplant to which they had been accustomed.

The first of Waterbeach's operational pilots to fly the new aircraft was OC Flying Wing, Wing Commander Mike Giddings, he being quickly followed by OC No 56 Squadron, Squadron Leader 'Twinkle' Storey, both men getting airborne on 22 February under the watchful eye of Supermarine test pilot David Morgan. Both pilots had a trouble-free flight, as did the Squadron's 'A' Flight Commander, 'Mac'

COURTESY CHRIS CHRISTIE

COURTESY PETER COLLINS/CHRIS CHRISTIE

Opposite page, above and below: The first Swift F.1, WK209, arrives on No 56 Squadron at RAF Waterbeach, 20 February 1954–to, of course, an excited and enthusiastic welcome. The extreme rear segment of the cockpit canopy of these early Swifts contained a suppressed aerial–hence the unpainted finish, contrasting with the High Speed Silver of the airframe proper; further suppressed aerials were located in the inboard leading edges of the wings (showing as dark horizontal strips in these photographs). VHF whip aerials were located atop the fuselage and beneath. The nose cone contained the aircraft's basic ranging radar equipment and, along the port side, the aperture for the gun camera.

McCaig, and his deputy, John Gledhill, shortly thereafter. John would be responsible for converting the 'A' Flight pilots first, while those on 'B' Flight continued to fly the Meteor.

With the winter weather and poor aircraft serviceability taking their toll, the transition programme was protracted. In February the three F.1s available

COURTESY CHRIS CHRISTIE

COCKPIT LAYOUT

SUPERMARINE SWIFT Mks 1 and 2

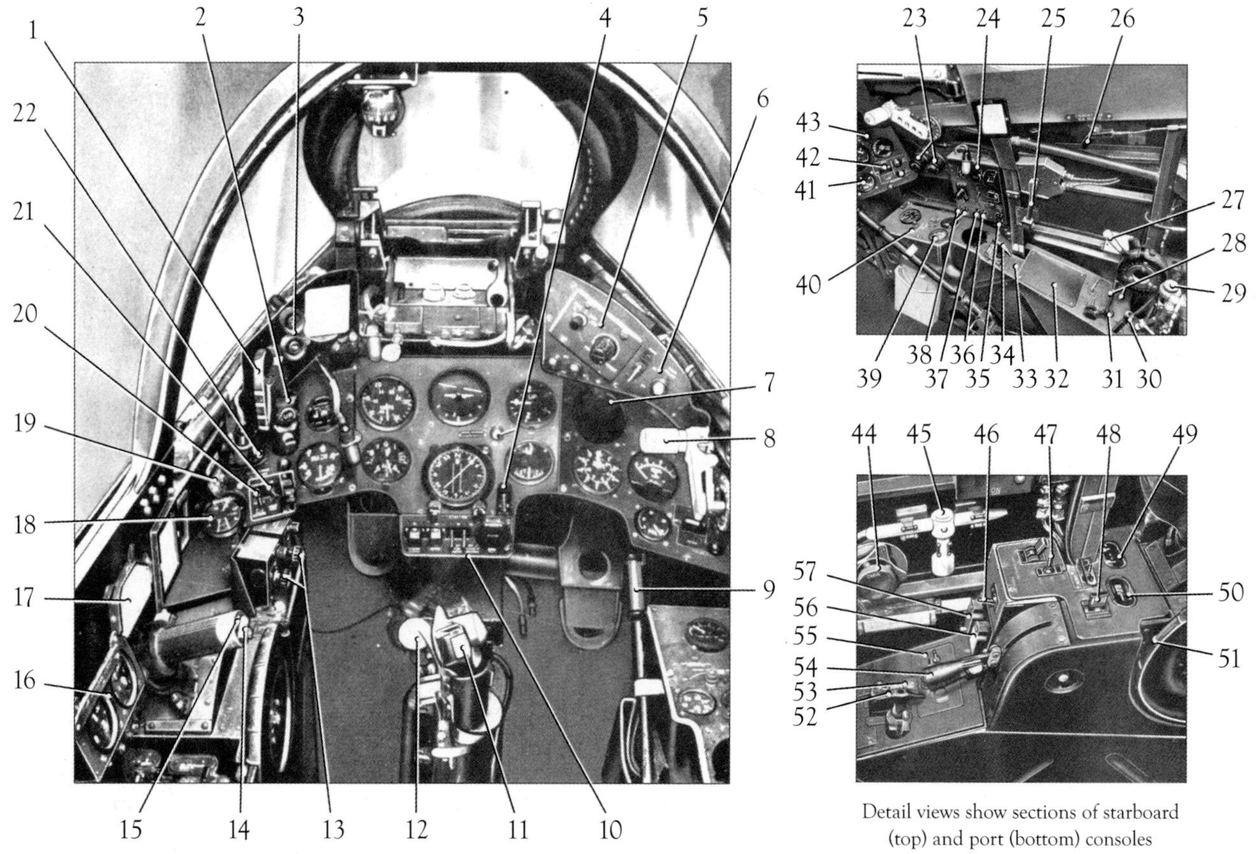

Detail views show sections of starboard (top) and port (bottom) consoles

Key to illustrations

1. Hood jettison control.
2. Undercarriage selector buttons (brake boost switch outboard of buttons).
3. Fire warning lights and extinguisher buttons.
4. Aileron power on/off switch and indicator.
5. Gyro gun sight selector dimmer control (generator failure indicators underneath).
6. Radar range on/off switch and indicator. (Note: When the cabin pressure warning light is fitted, it replaces the radar magnetic indicator, which is then repositioned above the radar range on/off switch.)
7. Position of DME (Rebecca Mk 7, ARI.5849) indicator (internal tanks fuel flow indicators fitted on right of indicator on aircraft subsequent to WK208).
8. Hood winding handle.
9. Hydraulic handpump.
10. Starter panel—left to right: starter master switch; ignition switch; fuel master switch; battery isolation switch; starter pushbutton.
11. Elevator trim control switch.
12. Artificial spring feel trim.
13. VHF controllers.
14. Flaps inching switch.
15. Press-to-transmit switch.
16. Main hydraulic accumulators air pressure gauges.
17. Hood jettison mechanism 'safe' indicator.
18. Triple pressure gauge.
19. Radar ranging target reject switch.
20. Fuel override switch.
21. Pressure head heater switch.
22. Flaps position indicator and limit setting switch (outboard of indicator).
23. Cockpit lamps dimmer switches.
24. Armament control panel.
25. Footstep control handle.
26. Hood seal emergency release.
27. LP cock lever.
28. Telebriefing warning light and call switch.
29. Anti-G system test button.
30. Emergency oxygen control.
31. Anti-G system on/off control.
32. DME panel location.
33. Position for hydraulic system audio warning 'On test/Off' switch.
34. Rudder bar adjustment control.
35. Cockpit pressure warning horn cut-out switch.
36. Emergency lamp switch.
37. Navigation lights switch.
38. G.45 camera on/off and aperture switches.
39. Cockpit altimeter.
40. Mk 17 demand oxygen regulator.
41. Oil pressure gauge.
42. Fuel balance switch and indicators.
43. Fuel pressure warning indicator.
44. Cockpit ventilator.
45. Ammunition tanks access key.
46. Rudder trim control switch.
47. Cockpit pressure and temperature controls.
48. Aileron trim switch.
49. Rudder and aileron trim position indicators.
50. Elevator trim position indicator.
51. Elevator emergency trim control.
52. Belly tank jettison control.
53. Elevator power on/off control.
54. HP cock lever and relight button.
55. IFF (Identification Friend or Foe) control panel.
56. Flaps emergency lowering pushbutton.
57. Undercarriage emergency lowering pushbutton.

COURTESY RICHARD CAREY

flew ten hours and in March five aircraft generated thirteen, but there was a marked improvement in April when Swift flying hours totalled 137. Then in May came the first of the Squadron's Swift accidents: 'Twinkle' Storey was forced to eject from a spin in WK209, and Flying Officer Neil Thornton was killed when one aileron locked on take-off and his aircraft rolled into the ground. This brought all Swift flying to a halt while modifications were made to the flight controls, selectors and warning system, but it would be the only fatal accident in a Swift during the aircraft's time on No 56. Albeit with very limited

AUTHOR'S COLLECTION

Left: Despite the problems afflicting the Swift, No 56 Squadron contributed five aircraft for the Battle of Britain Fly Past over London in September 1954—four F.2s and an F.1.
Below: A further view of the Squadron's first Swift, WK209, chocked and with intake blanks fitted following its arrival on the Station. A pilot is seated in the cockpit, and the officer on the left contemplating the new equipment is believed to be Mike Giddings, Wing Commander Flying at Waterbeach.

experience on the aircraft, the pilots of 'A' Flight were quick to conclude that the F.1 was unlikely to become an acceptable high level fighter—although they extolled its virtues at low level.

With the Squadron now down to four F.1s, only 44 hours were recorded when flying resumed in August, during which WK213 was lost when Flying Officer John Hobbs ejected successfully after failing to get his nosewheel down for landing. Modifications to the undercarriage followed, as a batch of F.2s arrived on the Squadron to bring the strength up to twelve aircraft in September. The F.2 was a disappointment; it did not handle well in the air, ten knots had to be added to the F.1's landing speed, and its serviceability was no better than that of its predecessor. A spate of hydraulic failures, affecting both variants, then led to a further grounding, although the Squadron was able to muster five aircraft to overfly London on Battle of Britain Day in 1954.

COURTESY PETER COLLINS

COURTESY CHRIS CHRISTIE

First and foremost, No 56 Squadron was required, at every opportunity, to give maximum publicity and visibility to the Swift, with flypasts and individual demonstrations before VIPs and at RAF Open Days. However, tactical training had now also begun in earnest, for the pilots to explore the fighting capabilities of the aircraft. They soon got used to the sensitive power controls, proving this by their progress in ranging and tracking with the gyro gun sight in demanding cine-camera exercises, but they found all manœuvres at high level, in battle formation and in tail chases difficult. The fighter had yet to be cleared to fire its guns. Then came another winter of bad weather, which again combined with poor serviceability to result in a monthly average of only 58 flying hours.

All in all, the first year of Swift operations, in the hands of average squadron pilots, had not been a success and, with both A&AEE and AFDS continuing to issue dire warnings on the likely efficacy of the aircraft in the high-level fighter rôle, even with developments in the pipeline, the Air Ministry decreed, on 15 March 1955, that all Swift flying at Waterbeach should cease. It is unlikely that anyone at Waterbeach disagreed with this decision, but several of the pilots retain fond memories of the aircraft. Chris Christie, for example, tried hard to get the best out of the aircraft, making good use of its spectacular acceleration, climb rate and unprecedented (for the time) top speeds. He and others were also impressed by the responsiveness of the power controls, the rate of roll and the effectiveness of the air brake/flap. They felt that most first-tour pilots would have had little difficulty flying the aircraft, but all agreed that it would be more at home in low-level operations. They were right.

Above: External checks completed, one of No 56 Squadron's pilots embarks for a flight in his Swift F.1. Martin-Baker Type 2G ejection seats were fitted to Swift F.1s, and these saved the lives of two pilots.
Below: The entire Squadron in July 1954, with a Swift to the right and one of the retained Gloster Meteors to the left.

COURTESY CHRIS CHRISTIE

Pride and Enthusiasm *Group Captain G. J. ('Twinkle') Storey*

The arrival of the Swift in February 1954 had been eagerly anticipated by the groundcrew. Although new equipment with associated problems was naturally a little daunting in the early days, it was not long before the groundcrew realised that they had a monster to deal with—hydraulic leaks and failures, control problems, random and obscure electrical faults *et al*—and the design failure to provide for a rapid aircraft turn-round did nothing to inspire groundcrew confidence in the aircraft as an operational fighter. They had an extremely frustrating and trying time in providing the few serviceable aircraft that they did achieve. It was their determination, resilience and loyalty that enabled the pilots to enjoy those very limited hours when the aircraft were available for flying. The sustained efforts of the groundcrew were truly outstanding.

It had been decided, before the aircraft arrived, that 'A' Flight would be converted first so that pilots could consolidate their initial Swift flying. However, because of the very poor availability of aircraft, it was soon realised that we could not proceed with 'B' Flight if we were to maintain safety standards. That was hard for the 'B' Flight pilots, who grudgingly accepted the situation. Towards the end of the Swift era, when withdrawal from service of the aircraft was likely, we were able to change that policy, and 'B' Flight joined the conversion programme before further Swift training was banned and the aircraft were flown away by our pilots to the MU.

Perhaps a measure of the difficulties we had faced was exemplified by the hours achieved during the period of fourteen months' squadron service. In the first six months there were only five Swift Mk 1 aircraft—and during that time the aircraft were grounded for some two months—although strength increased to eleven aircraft, both Mk 1 and Mk 2, in the last six months. One must also allow for the fact that flying times were recorded from wheels rolling to touch-down. Nonetheless, a total of 720 hours was not exactly outstanding, and the highest individual flying time was a mere 68 hours. However, we did convert thirty-four Squadron pilots and provided flights for nearly as many 'outside' pilots, including the CAS.

Happily, aircrew morale remained high throughout the Swift era. The loss of Neil Thornton, a popular and enthusiastic young pilot, was a sad but temporary 'blip' only, and was something which occurred elsewhere in the fighter world; fortuitously, it was the only fatality. However, that is not to overlook two ejections and the frequency of incidents, many of them serious, that the pilots experienced all too often in the air. Of course, as with the groundcrew, the pilots had many disappointments and frustrations, but their keenness to get into the cockpit never abated. The aircraft had handling problems but it was, nevertheless, exciting to fly as it provided a speed, a rate of roll, powerful air brakes, etc., far superior to those of its predecessors. It should be remembered that, at that time in particular, there was great kudos in being on No 56 Squadron: it was the first RAF squadron to be equipped with the first British swept-wing fighter. It was exhilarating, and pride and enthusiasm in those circumstances would be felt by any keen young fighter pilot—and they were.

Unfortunately there was another side of the coin: the Swift arrived with an operating height limitation of 25,000 feet. No doubt some aircraft strayed above that level, only to confirm to the pilot that there little point in exceeding the limitation. The aircraft could not execute more than a gentle turn, even at that height, without experiencing buffeting. Fighter manœuvres were out of the question.

The Swift had been put into squadron service far too early under the political pressure to have a British swept-wing fighter in the front line (the US-designed F-86 was already in RAF squadron service). It was a significant

COURTESY CHRIS CHRISTIE

Left : CO Squadron Leader 'Twinkle' Storey (far left) with (left to right) Flight Lieutenant 'Mac' McCaig, Flying Officer Al Martin and Flying Officer Al ('Harv') Harvie of No 56 Squadron. 'Mac' MacCaig—whose 'bone dome' carries a 'Fiji' emblem (a reference to his nickname when serving on No 249 Squadron) rather than the Squadron device—recalls that his was a unique position within the Squadron: 'I was given the rare privilege of commanding a complete, composite and independent RAF fighter flight within his [the CO's] unit. . . . One of my main responsibilities was to flight-familiarise pilots and see if it could be done with little briefing on the ground and myself in the ATC tower as an R/T safety check controller once the solo pilot was airborne. . . . Lots of gallons of sweat every time they flew!'

advance on the Meteor and Vampire, both technically and in terms of performance, but, unfortunately, it had been introduced into the Squadron at the same time as the Swift's flight trials were taking place at Boscombe Down. There is no doubt that the Squadron missed the benefit of the extensive trials that a new aircraft normally undergoes before being released for squadron service. Moreover, there was not the support of the highly efficient Flight Safety organisation as exists today. Reports on incidents occurring at A&AEE, at the Central Fighter Establishment and on the Squadron were often not disseminated or were not circulated with the promptness required. Hence incidents occurred that might have been avoided and problems arose that could have been identified earlier.

However, throughout the period of the Swift, in spite of the lack of serviceable aircraft and its disappointing performance as a fighter, there was never a lack of confidence with the pilots. We were not glad to see the aircraft go—reverting to Meteors was retrograde—but it was realised that the aircraft was a complete failure in the air defence rôle.

After all the many difficulties that the Squadron had experienced, there was a happy ending: two months after the departure of the Swifts, we re-equipped with the Hunter Mk 5 in May 1955.

Right: Meanwhile, trials and testing of the Swift continued at West Raynham in the hands of the AFDS, who did not finalise their report on the aircraft until late June 1954. It came as no surprise to those on No 56 that fulsome praise for the Swift was notable chiefly for its absence.

We Lucky Few *Flight Lieutenant Richard Carrey*

At the beginning of 1954 No 56 Squadron was a standard day fighter unit, based at RAF Waterbeach, just north of Cambridge. We had 22 Meteor Mk 8 day fighters and about 35 pilots, many of whom, like me, were 'first tourists'. The Boss, Squadron Leader 'Twinkle' Storey, gave us the news in January that we were to undertake the intensive flying trials of the Swift, and the first aircraft started arriving at the end of February. 'Mac' McCaig, the Flight Commander of 'A' Flight, was chosen to be the trials leader, which meant that I, as a member of his Flight, would be one of those getting an early chance to get some swept-wing experience. 'B' Flight in the meantime would be maintaining the Squadron's rôle as an operational unit.

We were not destined to become 'test pilots', of course, as the purpose of the trial was more down to earth: the aims were simply to operate the aircraft, to gain experience of any problems that might arise, and, as far as the groundcrew were concerned, to devise servicing schedules, and assess the sort of serviceability the Swifts could achieve and the kind of spares backing that they needed. All they wanted from us was to 'Get airborne, stay up as long as you can, and—please—come back serviceable.' They were certainly in for a few surprises!

The Air Fighting Development Squadron at West Raynham were concurrently carrying out the evaluation of the aircraft as a fighter, and, until their report was published, No 56 were operating on a very restricted clearance—there was to be no flying above 25,000 feet, and there was a speed restriction of 0.9M/550 knots.

As a fairly lowly member of the Flight, it was some time before I would get my turn, but we all did a little conversion course, run by Johnnie Gledhill, the Deputy Flight Commander. It was only in retrospect that I appreciated how well 'Mac' McCaig and Johnnie ran the whole project with so little in the way of teaching aids. There was no simulator nor even a cardboard cockpit to help us familiarise

COURTESY PHILIP JARRETT

ourselves. Very few copies of the 'roneo'd' typescript Provisional Pilot's Notes had been provided, and after all the 'must-haves' like the Station Commander and Wingco Flying had their copies, only one was left for all the other pilots. As the book was classified as Secret, this of course was locked in the adjutant's safe and needed to be signed out each time one needed to consult it. Luckily, my little daughter's favourite comic, *Mickey Mouse Weekly*, published a centre page picture of 'A Modern Jet's Cockpit', which happened to be the very cockpit photograph in the Pilot's Notes—it even retained the word 'Secret' stamped at the top and bottom of each view! So I was able to use her comic to learn the layout of the various switches and dials and to memorise the checklists and drills.

It was May by the time I got to the top of the list, and was looking forward to starting my conversion. I was just re-joining the circuit in a Meteor on the afternoon of 13 May when I heard the voice of Neil Thornton, the pilot immediately ahead of me in the list, calling up for take-off, already on his second conversion flight. I held off for a while to watch him depart. Imagine my horror as I saw him take off, slowly roll over and crash in the fen near Soham. He was killed instantly. Only 22 years old, Neil was a good friend and a popular member of the Squadron, and his death was a great loss to us all.

Neil's accident had been caused by a defect in the powered control system to the ailerons. The Swifts were immediately grounded until a modification to give a much more positive means of selecting the power control system could be installed. After the aircraft had all been modified and air-tested by the Supermarine test pilots, and the qualified pilots had all had a refresher, I finally made my first flight in September, and I completed the six-sortie conversion programme over the next few days.

The pilot climbed into the Swift Mk 1 using a retractable footstep and toe holes, rather like the Meteor but, for some

Below: The Mk 1 flight line during some inclement weather at Waterbeach. Hydraulic leakages seemed to afflict Supermarine aircraft more than those of other manufacturers (the Navy's Scimitar had a similar characteristic), and drums to catch the inevitable drips were usually well in evidence, as here. The Squadron's famous red and white chequerboards have now been applied, both to the fuselage and to the wing tips.

COURTESY PHILIP JARRETT

COURTESY PHILIP JARRETT

COURTESY CHRIS CHRISTIE

Left, upper: A Swift F.1 taxies out to the runway at Waterbeach. Left, lower, and main image: Further views of No 56 Squadron's Swift F.1s at Waterbeach, as line crews prepare the aircraft for flying. Right: No 56 Squadron personnel on 24 June 1954: (front row, left to right) Flight Sergeants Mitchell, Herbert, Nisbet and Freddie Jacques, with Gretel keeping an eye on them; (second row, from left) Flight Lieutenants Webster, John Gledhill and 'Mac' McCaig, Squadron Leader 'Twinkle' Storey (CO), Captain Jack Bodie USAF and Flight Lieutenant 'Hoppy' Hoppitt; (centre row, from left) Flying Officers Al Martin, John Hobbs, Dave Stringer, Ken Mills, Mike Withey, Chris Christie, Hugh Crawley, Ray Fenning, Roy Chitty and Bill Sykes, and Flight Lieutenant Ivor Simmons; (seated on wing, from left) Flying Officers Stu Drury, Jock Byrne, Dick Carrey and Tony Sumner; and (standing on wing) Flying Officers Pat Gower (left) and Mike Daulby. The Swift in the background lacks its ejection seat.

reason, on the starboard side. Single-seater pilots generally mount from the nearside, like cavalrymen, so we blamed this departure from custom on the aircraft's 'fishhead' ancestry. Thanks to my 'Mickey Mouse' photograph, I found the cockpit familiar and was soon taxying out. The wide-track, softly sprung undercarriage made the experience feel quite luxurious, and this was one of the features of the Swift that we missed when we converted to Hunters the following summer.

Even opening up to max rpm against the brakes, Waterbeach's 2,000-yard runway, with the Ely road at the end, looked awfully short, but the take-off was rapid and there was no feeling of over-controlling on the ailerons. Remembering to raise the flaps was the next thing, and soon we were climbing away at 415 knots at a great rate. The conversion exercises were quite short but left little time for individual 'exploration of the envelope'; later we were able to get more familiar with the aircraft and its funny ways.

There was no jealousy or ill-feeling shown by the members of 'B' Flight towards us lucky few, for several reasons: first, the Boss had made it plain that everybody would get his go in the Swift sooner or later; secondly, both flights co-operated in order to fulfil the operational task of the Squadron; and thirdly, flying the Meteor, obsolescent as it was, was so much fun. The first part of a typical Meteor sortie, until the ventral tank was empty, would be devoted

COURTESY TONY BUTLER

COURTESY RICHARD CARREY

to battle formation or, more often, to practice low flying in our local playground, Low Level Area Uxbridge One—otherwise known as the whole of East Anglia. Here there were steam trains puffing across Breckland , just asking to be strafed, the Broads and woodland for low-level navigation and 'Rat and Terrier' exercises, and a multitude of disused airfields for practising forced-landing techniques. There were so many airfields, in fact, that it was believed that from 3,000 feet and 300 knots a Meteor pilot should be able to close the throttles anywhere in East Anglia and carry out a low approach, wheels down, into wind, on a runway of sorts with a fair degree of certainty. So, although the Swift was heavily restricted as far as high-speed, high-altitude operational flying was concerned, there was plenty going on lower down. Over the next six months I flew the Swift on 43 occasions, and enjoyed each enormously. The sorties were varied—aerobatics, formation flying, low flying, forced landings or high level cross-countries. The cross-country flying was necessary because the Pilot's Notes had been published without any flight planning data or fuel consumption figures, and so we were writing our own.

At high level the Swift was disappointing. Even at 25,000 feet, it was difficult to fly in battle formation. When the formation started a turn, the aircraft on the inside would try to stay on the inside as long as possible, diving slightly to pass well ahead of the leader before losing ground on the outside of the turn, finishing up in line abreast on the

COURTESY RICHARD CARREY/ROY RIMINGTON

Left: A print of a No 56 Squadron six-aircraft echelon—three F.1s and three F.2s—autographed by the pilots: 'Twinkle' Storey, 'Mac' McCaig, Dick Carrey, Al Martin, Roy Rimington and Pat Gower.

other side. It was all too easy for the speed to build up in the dive to 0.91M or more, and, as the elevators became completely ineffective above this speed, the unfortunate wingman would find himself flying off at a tangent, never to catch up with his leader again. Where the Hunter had an electrically trimming, variable-incidence tailplane, and a fully powered elevator, the Swift had a subsonic-type fixed tailplane with an elevator that was only power-assisted and fitted with a traditional trim tab. All-flying tailplanes were promised for both types of aircraft, but the Hunter was much closer to being a finished operational fighter aircraft.

The other two failings of the Swift—and of the Hunter Mk 1, if to a much lesser degree—were the pitch-up problem when flying close to the stall at high altitude, and the propensity of the Avon RA.7 to surge at low ambient temperatures, again at high altitude. Pitch-up was a phenomenon related to the swept wing, and so was completely unfamiliar to 'straight wing pilots'. As the wing tips stalled before the inboard sections of the wing, the centre of lift moved rapidly inboard and forward; thus, if the aircraft was turning, the turn would tighten uncontrollably. To cure this characteristic it was proposed to increase the chord of the outer part of the wing, giving the leading edge the so-called 'sawtooth'—but this would not be fitted until the Mk 4 version of the aircraft.

The Swift had a neat little gauge in the cockpit to deal with the surge problem, the surge/rpm gauge, which measured absolute temperature (outside air temperature modified by forward airspeed). If the temperature was low the needle moved into the red sector, where the maximum surge-free rpm was displayed. If the pilot did not immediately throttle back, descend into warmer air or increase forward speed (preferably all three), there would be A Very Loud Bang, probably a flame-out and possibly damage to the engine. An ashen face and a faraway look on a recently returned pilot showed only too plainly that he had experienced a surge on his last trip!

When the AFDS report was published, it confirmed the general impressions formed on the Squadron: the Swift had been hurried into service before the 'bugs' had been shaken out. Although solutions to the main faults had been proposed, they had not yet been proved in practice. In fact, the Swift was a bit of an ugly duckling, while the Hawker Hunter was already a swan. There was more. AFDS were unimpressed by the rate of turn at high altitude, which, it was felt, was not materially improved in the later marks. A high-altitude day fighter that lacks manœuvrability simply will not do, and the decision to abandon the trial came as no surprise.

The farewell six-ship formation flight on 11 March 1955 produced some nice photographs, the pictures being taken by a Meteor 9 pilot from No 226 OCU based at Stradishall. This was almost my last Swift sortie. We said goodbye to the Swift without too much regret, and went back to life as a normal squadron. The groundcrew had struggled against great difficulties for over a year. They had had to become

COURTESY PHILIP JARRETT

COURTESY ROY RIMINGTON

COURTESY PHILIP JARRETT

Top: The Squadron's yellow and black vintage Rolls-Royce, complete with 'phœnix rising' emblem and flanking red and white chequers on the door. The vehicle was funded by the pilots and utilised adventurously during off-duty hours. The Swift in the background, WK212, has had its tail code letter applied but not yet its squadron markings.
Above: F.1 WK209/'B', in full squadron markings, taxies past a Devon and a Meteor. The venue is, probably, Waterbeach and the occasion, probably, the AOC's inspection.
Below: The Squadron flight line at Waterbeach following the reception of some Swift Mk 2s in the late summer of 1954. The Mk 2s brought with them double the firepower but extra weight as a result: the advantage was theoretical as the weapons were destined never to be fired, while the additional weight detracted still further from the Swift's questionable capability as an interceptor.

acquainted with a more complex aircraft than the Meteor very rapidly. Like its illustrious Supermarine predecessor the Spitfire, the Swift was not designed with ease of servicing in mind, and the constant procession of minor snags, combined with a chronic shortage of spares, made their task even harder. In June, to universal rejoicing, No 56 Squadron became a Hunter squadron, and within six months the Swift had been reborn in its new fighter-reconnaissance rôle.

It would be nice to think that the hard work put in by No 56 Squadron groundcrew and pilots made a contribution to the aircraft's ultimate successs.

Mixed Feelings *Squadron Leader Jock Byrne* MBE QCVSA

I was stationed at Waterbeach from December 1953 until July 1956 and so was present from the transition from Meteor 8s to Swifts and then on to Hunters. The conversion course consisted of a cockpit procedures check accompanied by three rather wearily delivered pieces of advice: 'Take-off speed is such-and-such; landing speed is such-and-such; and don't stall it!' There were of course no dual aircraft (except the Vampire, for instrument ratings), and this is the way things were done—absolutely fabulous! The airfield at that time was home to No 56 and No 63 Squadrons, equipped with Meteors when I arrived, and, from spring 1955, No 253 with Venom night fighters.

There was, of course, absolute elation amongst the Squadron when No 56 learned that it was to receive the new Swift—this was, after all, the first swept-wing jet. The elation dimmed a little, however, when we learned about the restrictions that were being placed on our flying (pleasant though the latter would prove to be). Officially, we were limited to 25,000 feet altitude and 0.9M (550 knots), although nobody really took much notice of this: certainly, greenhouse windows were shattered from time to time! In fact, many of the pilots took the aircraft through the sound barrier in a dive—on the principle that if you are expected to fly an aircraft in combat, you really ought to find out all about it!

As a fighter, however, the Swift did not follow the script. It suffered from pitch-up, the aircraft being unable properly to execute a tight turn; had it put up against a MiG-15, for example, it would have been totally outclassed in this respect—simply unable to compete. The general handling was quite acceptable, although the switch from power to manual control was difficult, requiring the pilot to reach awkwardly behind the seat to effect the transition (in the later Hunter, the changeover required merely the flick of a switch). Thus if one wing happened to be in power and one in manual, there was real trouble if the switch could not be located quickly—especially if the aircraft was on finals.

We had lost one of our number during this time, a young pilot, when one of his ailerons unlocked just after take-off and he had no chance of controlling the aircraft, nor of ejecting. The Boss, 'Twinkle' Storey, had to eject when his aircraft began to spin uncontrollably as he was carrying out some exploratory flying. There were a number of other 'hiccups', including an incident when OC Flying, Wing Commander Mike Giddings, suffered aileron problems when switching from power to manual in the circuit, although his experience as a test pilot enabled him to regain control and land safely.

When the Mk 2 came along—only a matter of months after the first Mk 1s had been issued, and on which, incidentally, I did most of my Swift flying—there was little difference. The Squadron spent its time evaluating the Swift's capabilities and trying to wring the best out of the airframe, so much so that the question of weapons practice never arose. There were mixed feelings when we learnt that we were to give up our Swifts after only a year or so of flying them, the degree of sadness at seeing them go tempered by the fact that we were to be re-equipped with the Hunter, which was streets ahead of its rival in terms of manœuvrability.

COURTESY ROY RIMINGTON

Above: Flying Officer (now Squadron Leader) Roy Rimington poses beside one of No 56 Squadron's Swift F.2s. This photograph affords a clear view of the paired cannon troughs beneath the F.2's main intakes, differentiating this mark from the F.1, which had single Aden cannon each side.
Below: Swift F.2 WK239 in September 1954; this was probably one of the aircraft that took part in the Battle of Britain Fly Past (see page 31). Apart from the gun armament and the paint finish, the principal difference between the Mk 1 and the Mk 2 was the latter's extended wing chord at the root. However, there were other distinguishing features, for example the configuration of the cooling intakes atop the fuselage.

COURTESY RICHARD CARREY

Waiting for Thicker Air *Air Vice-Marshal Peter Collins CB AFC BA*

It was February 1955. I was in the final months of my first tour as a fighter pilot on No 63 Squadron based at Waterbeach and No 56 Squadron, our sister squadron on the base, had just received their first deliveries of the Swift Mk 1 and Mk 2 and their pilots were beginning trials of this new swept-wing fighter. The RAF was then a much larger and less regulation-driven organisation than today's shrunken air force, and it was quite normal for pilots to fly different types when the opportunity arose without having to complete a conversion course. My squadron was equipped with the Meteor Mk 8, on which I had accumulated some 700 hours, and I was one of the lucky ones to be offered the chance to fly the Swift.

My familiarisation sortie was on a Mk 2, WK221, on 27 February. I suppose I must have read the Pilots' Notes (assuming they existed at that time) and one of the No 56 Squadron pilots would have supervised my strapping-in, cockpit checks and start-up before the hood was closed and I taxied away. Then I was on my own. The sortie consisted of little more than a climb to medium altitude, some handling to get the feel of the aircraft, perhaps a few aeros and then a recovery to base for a couple of circuits and overshoots before landing. I remember little of the flight itself. The early Swift was not excitingly powered, but it was considerably faster than the Meteor and I enjoyed flying it. In the circuit the aircraft handled well and the landing posed no problems.

The next day I had my second sortie after an hour in the familiar Meteor doing aerobatics and 'bouncing' a battle formation of four of my No 63 Squadron colleagues to check their awareness and defensive response. This time it was in a Swift Mk 1, WK 207, and I was authorised for a full work-out, including a supersonic dive. Again, at this distance in time, much of the detail of the flight has been forgotten. I remember it included a practice forced-landing (PFL)—a standard precaution when flying a single-engined machine. You cut the throttle at, say, 5,000 feet, looked for a suitable field and coasted down to it, aiming to fly a high downwind leg and finals, lowering gear and flaps as required, all without touching the power, then overshooting at the last moment. No problems there, and I climbed up for what would be for me the real excitement of the sortie, the supersonic dive—something I had never experienced before.

The Swift climbed rather faster than the Meteor and I reached 42,000 feet in less than ten minutes (I think), then, after clearing the area below me, I rolled over into a steep dive and hurtled earthward watching the Machmeter. Soon it registered just over Mach 1 and I eased back on the stick to recover. Nothing happened! Soon I had the stick right back in my stomach with the aircraft still in its downward path. Eventually, at below 30,000 feet, it began to respond and both the aircraft and my stomach resumed normal flight condition. We later coined the expression 'waiting for thicker air' when describing the Swift's supersonic dive performance. It was, in fact, indicative of the aircraft's inadequate tailplane authority, one of the shortcomings that led ultimately to its abandonment as a high-level interceptor.

Comparisons with the Meteor are relatively meaningless. This was a new-generation swept-wing fighter and we expected it to feel markedly superior. It was certainly a lot faster, its climb performance was superior and, at low level certainly, it was more agile. I was glad to have flown it, but I did not especially envy my mates on No 56 their rôle as a Swift squadron. And so it proved. At least one fatality and a couple of ejections were, I think, to occur before the whole thing was called off in favour of the Hunter, destined to become the RAF's iconic swept-wing fighter. Meanwhile I was off to convert to night fighters and a future which would include the delta-winged Javelin and eventually the Lightning—the finest of them all.

COURTESY RICHARD CARREY/CHRIS CHRISTIE

Left and right: As the first 'swept-wing squadron', No 56 were tasked with a number of sorties that, while undeniably useful from the point of view of training, were flown primarily for the benefit of public relations (and, no doubt, to impress potential foes). They were also the result of some sterling work by the groundcrews, since rarely were six serviceable Swifts available at one time. These photographs were taken on one of these sorties, and that on the right, in particular, shows the extended inboard leading edges of the (camouflaged) Mk 2's wings.

COURTESY PHILIP JARRETT

COURTESY PHILIP JARRETT

'Stop That!' *Squadron Leader Roy Rimington*

The first Swifts to be introduced for operational flying—Mk 1s—were delivered to No 56 Squadron at Waterbeach in early 1954. Because of the shortage in numbers it was decided to convert the pilots of 'A' Flight from the Meteor to the Swift first while 'B' Flight continued to fly the Meteors. I was fortunate to be a young Flying Officer on 'A' Flight at the time. There was no simulator nor dual-control aircraft, and training aids were very limited; in fact, I think the Pilot's Notes were in a draft form before the little blue book was printed. We were naturally very excited at the thought of flying this new generation fighter with swept wings and the potential to travel faster than sound. Little did we know of the frustrations and disappointments that were to follow.

We were very impressed by the performance figures and the sleek lines compared to the Vampire and Meteor. One thing that was rather strange was the size of the control column grip, referred to by Peter Thorne as 'The Elephant Knob'. We were used to the spade control of the early Vampires and Meteors and the slim control column of the later variants. It was explained that the size was necessary to hold the numerous buttons and switches plus all the wiring. However, it was not very comfortable to use, and not possible to grip completely around its circumference. Although the same control column was used on the Mk 2 it was, fortunately, changed by the time we reached the Mk 5.

The first flight in a Mk 1 was quite memorable, even though it was nearly sixty years ago. Apart from the huge increase in power, the aileron control was extremely light. One quickly got used to this, however, and the aileron power control of the Swift was one of its greatest assets. The circuit and landing was fairly straightforward once one got used to the higher approach and landing speeds. We were also very impressed by the combined flap and air brake. In the air brake setting the device could be used at any speed incrementally down to a maximum of 30 degrees, which was reached, I believe, at about 400 knots. There was then a further setting which would allow full flap to be selected for landing. It is interesting to note that the same configuration was intended to be used on the early Hunter, but the trim changes were unacceptable and it was abandoned. The Hunter then had the extra air brake fitted below the fuselage.

Our training was hampered by serviceability problems, and this became very frustrating for us. We naturally wanted to get on with flying the aircraft and to get to know it, but there were very few aircraft to fly. I achieved a total of 5 hours 10 minutes' flying in seven sorties in the first month, with a complete lack of continuation between sorties. Fortunately we still kept a few Meteors on the Flight, so we could keep our hand in. I also had a Vampire T.11 to use for instrument flying training. In the year that we had the Swifts there was no month when I had more flying hours on Swifts than on other aircraft. Our flying was timed to the nearest minute by records of take-off and landing kept in Air Traffic Control instead of leaving the recording of times to the pilot. This pedantic approach was typical of the over-reaction to the introduction of swept-wing aircraft instead of just treating it as a natural progression: the transition was certainly no greater than the earlier one from propeller-driven to jet-engined aircraft.

In April we had the only fatal accident when Neil Thornton experienced control failure and rolled into the ground soon after take-off. It was his second sortie in the Swift and he was probably not fully conversant with the power control system. One selected power electrically by switch before take-off, and although the aircraft might feel 'in power' one had to confirm that it was locked in by reference to the black-and-white 'dolls' eyes'. If they were white, then the controls were not safely locked in the 'power' position and could fail at any time. This would cause the control to lock

Left: Another of the photographs taken during the six-aircraft formation exercise depicted on pages 42–43.
Below: WK242, a Swift Mk 2. The wing tips, as well as the fuselage sides, carried the Squadron chequers. The raked call-sign on the fin was also finished in red and white.

COURTESY PHILIP JARRETT

COURTESY JOCK BYRNE

solid, and the only resort was to deselect or switch off the power control and revert to manual control. This would require split-second thinking, of course, and simulator training for this kind of emergency would have been invaluable. It was not certain that this was the cause of the crash, however, and as a result the aircraft were grounded for modifications to the power control selectors. This took about three months, during which time we continued flying the Meteors. The modification consisted of a rather crude mechanical selector for the ailerons on the left side of the cockpit just above the throttle. It was certainly no easier, or faster, to use than the electrical switch but was considered safer than relying on electrics. The Hunter had similar aileron power controls, also with an electrical selector switch and 'dolls' eyes'. Although there were incidents of controls locking, it was not considered necessary to modify them to a mechanical selection.

In September the first of our Mk 2 Swifts arrived. There were minor differences, such as the extensions to the

Above: Officers of No 56 Squadron photographed in January 1955: (front row, left to right) Flying Officer Tony Sumner, Flight Lieutenant 'Hoppy' Hoppitt, Flight Lieutenant 'Mac' McCaig, Squadron Leader 'Twinkle' Storey (CO), Captain Clint Gillespie USAF and Flight Lieutenant Ivor Simmons; (back row, left to right) Flying Officers Dave Stringer, Ted Clowes, Pat Warne, Ray Fenning, Mike Chitty, Mike Daulby, Ken Mills, (obscured—unknown), Jock Byrne, Pat Gower, Hector Munro, Mike Withey, Stu Drury, Hugh Crawley, Bill Sykes, Roy Rimington, Chris Christie, Al Harvie, Dick Carrey, Tony Harris and John Hobbs.

inboard leading edges of the wings, but, generally, the handling characteristics were the same. However, the serviceability must have improved because I note from my logbook that I flew twelve Swift sorties in six consecutive days without flying another aircraft type. By this time we were flying regularly in formation and getting close to our operational rôle. I think we even managed to get eight aircraft airborne for a battle formation exercise. I do remember one occasion, when I was flying on the wing and, being fascinated by the rate of roll of this aircraft, I was seeing how fast I could roll it while maintaining battle formation position

COURTESY ROY RIMINGTON

Above: Roy Rimington disembarks from Swift Mk 2 WK240 on 15 March 1955—for the very last time, as he has just completed the final official flight on type for No 56 Squadron.
Below: Take-off from Waterbeach for the formation exercise depicted on pages 42–44. The sixth Swift is out of shot, to the left.

at about 150 yards. Since we were flying operationally we had strict radio silence, but just after one roll there were two abrupt words—'Stop that!'—from 'Mac' McCaig, who must have glanced round at the wrong moment.

I was airborne in a Mk 2 on 15 March 1955 when the order came through to ground all Swifts since they were being taken out of service. I was told of this by Air Traffic Control and warned to expect a photographer to meet me on landing. I remember being disappointed that this was going to be the end of a rather exciting period.

There is no doubt that the Swift was a failure as a high-level interceptor fighter, but it was not a failure as an aircraft *per se* and certainly not dangerous as is the normal misconception. I have had many people remark to me, 'Aren't you lucky to be alive?' on hearing that I flew the early Swift. However, contrary to popular rumour, we only had one fatal accident, and this was probably preventable. We did have incidents but most were, again, preventable. I doubt if the accident rate was any worse than that for any other recently introduced new aircraft, and from my own recollection it was certainly not as high as in the early days of the Meteor. The Swift was rushed into service since we were lacking a swept-wing aircraft at a time when other nations were getting them into service and we were still in a dangerous 'Cold War' period.

The Swift Mk 5 was a more finished product even though it was basically the same aircraft. For a start, the oversized control column grip was replaced by a much more manageable one similar to that of the Hunter. Reheat was fitted to the Mk 114 engine, which was not only useful operationally but was essential in some conditions when taking off with a full ventral tank The power controls were still selected mechanically, but the selectors were built into the side of the lower part of the instrument panel where they were easily accessible. The wings had 'sawtooth' leading edges instead of wing fences, which increased the wing area and improved manœuvrability. The aircraft also had a variable-incidence tailplane and a clear-view Perspex canopy which improved all-round vision. For its rôle in fighter-reconnaissance it was fitted with three Vinten F.95 oblique-facing cameras and retained two 30mm Aden cannon (which, finally, we could use).

The Mk 5 was ideally suited to the low-level reconnaissance rôle. It was stable and comfortable to fly at all speeds and as low as we needed. And, contrary to popular rumour, it was very manœuvrable at low level. This was helped with the use of reheat and the very effective combined flap/air brake. Moreover, the aileron control was second to none at the time. We achieved excellent results in air gunnery both on the flag at Sylt and on air-to-ground targets, which showed the Mk 5 to be a very stable gun platform. I do not think that we fired the guns above 15,000 feet, but then we were never expected to.

The Swift had a bad reputation and was much maligned, often by those with no experience of it, but personally I enjoyed flying it and consider the Mk 5 to be the best in its rôle at the time.

RENAISSANCE

Group Captain Nigel Walpole OBE BA

WHAT Fighter Command lost, with the failure of the Swift as an air defence fighter, the RAF's front line in Germany gained, with an aircraft able to fulfil an urgent need to replace the ageing Meteor F.R.9 in the fighter reconnaissance rôle. Whereas the Hunter F.R.10 was seemingly the best choice for this purpose, it would be some years before production capacity at Hawker could be diverted to that variant, and in the meantime a version of the Swift could provide an interim solution. Moreover, a large number of Swifts had been, or were being, produced that were now surplus to requirements, and they could be converted rapidly for use in the new rôle. Indeed, the first F.R.5s joined the RAF only eight months after the aircraft was declared redundant as a fighter.

So it was that extensive modifications were made to a Swift F.4, WK272, to evaluate its potential as a high-speed, low-level, fair-weather, camera-equipped, armed reconnaissance fighter. The aircraft's wing incorporated 'sawtooth' leading edges, thereby improving its manœuvrability, the fin was enlarged to give better directional stability and a clear-view canopy was fitted, to give better all-round visibility. What would become the Swift F.R.5 was driven by a reheated Avon 114 engine, giving 7,175 pounds of thrust dry and 9,450 pounds in reheat, at sea level, and 220 pounds of additional fuel could be made available from within a detachable ventral tank. The specialist FR rôle equipment consisted of three Vinten F.95 oblique cameras and associated accessories, optimised for low level, and a wire recorder to record visual sightings by the pilot. Unlike most contemporary aircraft of its type (for example, the Republic RF-84F) there would be no vertical cameras or viewfinder for the pilot to perfect his photography: aiming the oblique cameras was expected to become second nature. To make way for the cameras, two of the original Swift's Aden cannon were removed, but the retention of the remaining two, and the gyro gun sight, gave the fighter a worthwhile defensive combat and air-to-ground capability. Above all, the aircraft was considered sufficiently robust to sustain the punishment it would receive at the very high speeds and ultra-low levels in training, which would help it survive the myriad defences it would face in the Central Region of Europe should war break out.

Peter Thorne, then a test pilot with A&AEE at Boscombe Down, was charged with evaluating WK272, in trials carried out in

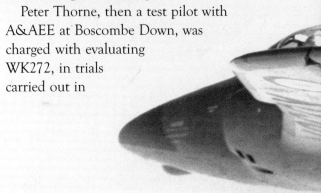

Below: WK200 was plucked from the F.1 delivery schedule by Supermarine and fitted with a new nose in connection with the proposed FR version of the Swift. It also featured a taller tailfin, but in most other respects it was a standard F.1, retaining the latter's straight wing leading edges, wing fences and even gun camera scoop.

MAIN IMAGE: BAE SYSTEMS

COURTESY TONY BUTTLER

conditions matched as closely as possible to those which might be expected in northern Germany, and based on the need for the aircraft to have a minimum radius of action of 150 nautical miles at 500 feet and speeds of 400–590 knots. The results, published in June 1955, were satisfactory. The aircraft could exceed the minimum range requirement in a typical operational profile, and it handled well on take-off, which usually required the use of reheat, aileron and elevator control remaining satisfactory throughout the speed range, albeit with the rudder becoming less responsive as speed increased. In reheat, it was possible for a 'clean' aircraft to reach speeds slightly in excess of 600 knots, and a maximum of 590 knots when fitted with the ventral tank. 'Dry', the maximum speeds were 565 knots and 550 knots, respectively. In power controls the F.R.5 handled well in the landing configuration, but touch-down speeds of about 130–135 knots could be critical on a 2,000-yard

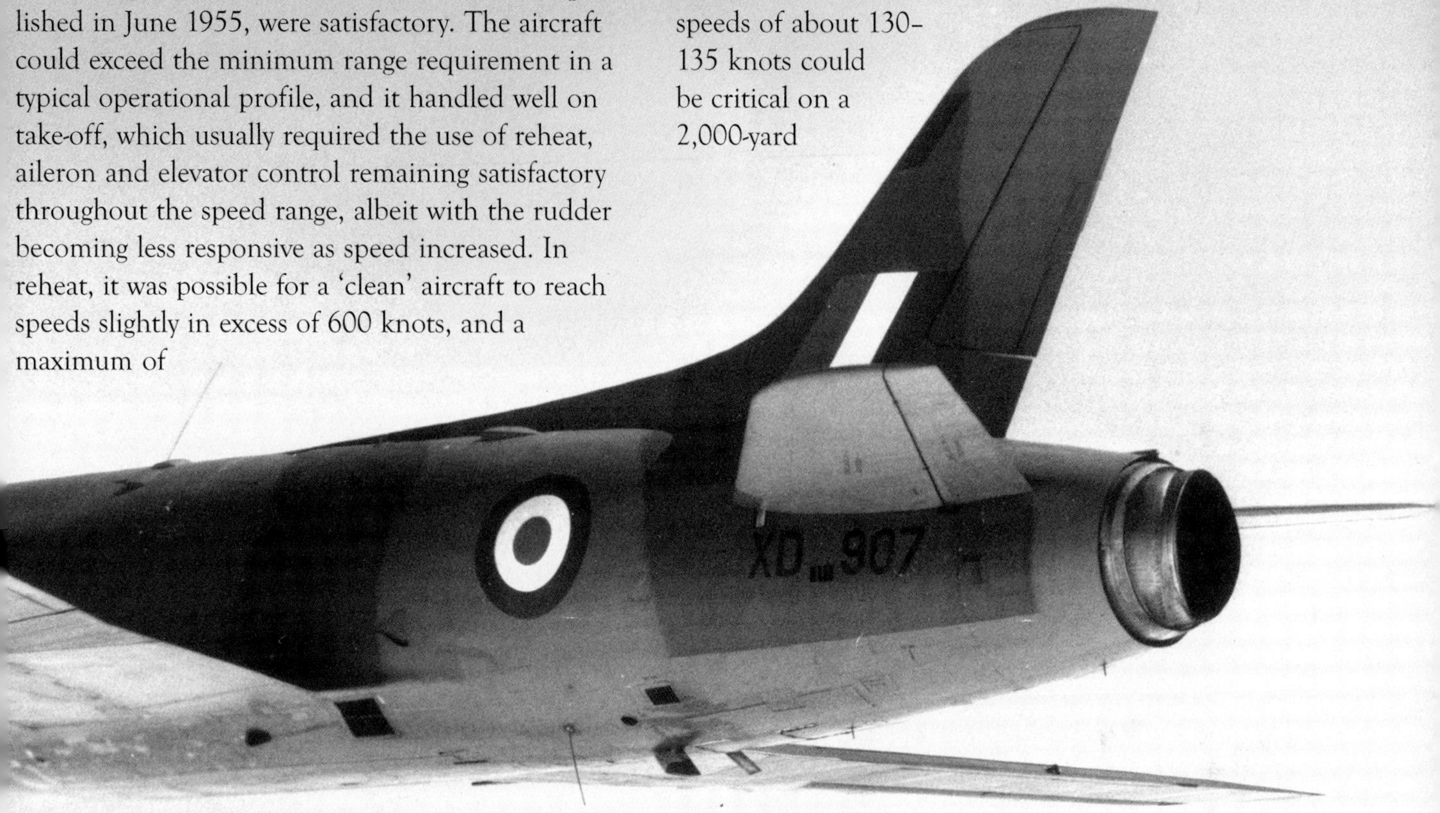

Above: A Swift Mk 5 on pre-delivery trials. As well as the redesigned nose and fin, this variant sported a yet further modified wing, incorporating 'dogtooth' (or 'sawtooth') leading edges as clearly seen here. The configuration of the reheat nozzle is also well illustrated in this photograph.

Below: XD904, another F.R. Mk 5. Those Mk 5s bearing serials prefixed with the letters 'WK' were for the most part conversions of Swift Mk 4s. This example has PRU Blue undersurfaces rather than High Speed Silver.

COURTESY PHILIP JARRETT

COURTESY PHILIP JARRETT

Left: A close view of the Swift Mk 5's 'sawtooth' wing leading edge, in a photograph that also shows that this mark dispensed with the chordwise wing fences evident on earlier variants.
Below: Newly completed F.R.5s awaiting delivery to the Royal Air Force. In evidence is the purpose-designed crew entry ladder, with cockpit entry now afforded from the port side of the aircraft. Notice, too, the linked blanks, protecting both the main intakes and the boundary layer air bleed intakes.
Right: A flight of Swift Mk 5s of No II (AC) Squadron. Only two of the aircraft have their full squadron markings, though the others have the black backgrounds to the fuselage markings applied. Call-signs are not yet present.

runway in wet, windless conditions, and landing in manual control in adverse conditions could be difficult.

A year later, the AFDS report on the F.R.5, rendered by selected pilots with recent front-line experience, generally supported the A&AEE findings, praising the aircraft as a gunnery and camera platform and commenting favourably upon its Maxaret brakes and three oblique cameras. Crucially, it found the aircraft sufficiently manœuvrable for the rôle at normal operating speeds, but warned against aggressive handling at speeds much below 350 knots, when the aircraft became generally 'less pleasant' to fly and could 'bite'; it also observed that a reversion to manual control at high speeds could produce a 'critical' situation, particularly if the aircraft was out of trim. The report went on to regret the very high fuel flow in reheat and certain engineering factors which were detrimental to rapid turn-rounds and would make servicing generally very difficult. Typically, the Avon engine had to be removed and replaced at an angle through the top of the fuselage, there were problems accessing most of the systems, and tyre changes and replenishment took time.

Ironically, the front line received its first F.R.5s five months before AFDS issued this report, and had already begun forming their own opinions of the efficacy of their new aircraft in FR. These aircraft had arrived on II Squadron, at RAF Geilenkirchen, on 23 February 1956. Germany's winter was not the best time of the year for the pilots to convert to a very different aircraft, and one that was likely to present the groundcrew with some unprecedented challenges—and so it proved. The first of the Squadron's pilots to get airborne in an F.R.5, on an air test on 6 April, was flight commander Ray Bannard, and the conversion programme progressed only slowly until the groundcrew became more familiar with the aircraft and serviceability improved sufficiently to facilitate the conversion of selected pilots from No 79 Squadron.

No 79 Squadron received the first of its F.R.5s, at RAF Wunstorf on 14 June 1956, its conversion programme benefiting significantly from the better

COURTESY PHILIP JARRETT

COURTESY PHILIP JARRETT

summer weather and the lessons learned by II Squadron over the previous four months. On both squadrons short but wholly adequate conversion programmes were completed without major incident, despite the lack of a dynamic flight simulator or dual-control Swift. In the autumn of that year No 79 moved to RAF Gütersloh, where it remained throughout the Swift's time in Germany, and operational rôle training was well under way on both squadrons.

SPECIFICATIONS

SUPERMARINE SWIFT Mks 1, 2 and 5

Manufacturer:	Supermarine Aircraft Company. Design and development at Hursley Park, Hampshire; production at South Marston, Wiltshire; test-flying at Chilbolton, Hampshire.
Chief Designer:	Joseph Smith.
Powerplant:	One Rolls-Royce Avon Mk 105 axial-flow turbojet developing 7,500lb (3,400kg, 33.36kN) static thrust at sea level or (Mk 5) Mk 114 developing 7,175lb (3,255kg, 31.92kN) dry and 9,450lb (4,286kg, 42.04kN) with reheat.
Dimensions:	Length overall 41ft 6in (12.65m), (Mk 5) 42ft 3in (12.88m); wing span 32ft 4in (9.85m); height 12ft 6in (3.81m), (Mk 5) 13ft 2in (4.01m) ; wing area (gross) 306.2 sq ft (28.45m^2), (Mk 2) 321.0 sq ft (29.82m^2), (Mk 5) 327.7 sq ft (30.44m^2).
Weights:	Empty 11,892lb (5,395kg), (Mk 2) 12,600lb (5,715kg), (Mk 5) 13,435lb (6,095kg); loaded 15,800lb (7,170kg), (Mk 2) 17,000lb (7,710kg), (Mk 5) 21,673 (9,830kg).
Armament:	Two (Mk 2 four) 30mm Aden cannon, plus (Mk 5) up to 2,000lb (905kg) of underwing stores.
Performance:	Maximum speed (clean, at sea level) 574kts (660mph, 1,062kph, Mach 0.87), (Mk 2) 590kts (680mph, 1,094kph, Mach 0.89), (Mk 5) 620kts (713mph, 1,147kph, Mach 0.94; initial climb rate 12,300ft/min (3,750m/min), (Mk 5) 14,660ft/min (4,470m/min); climb to 40,000ft (12,200m) (clean) 5.16min, (Mk 5) 4.69min; service ceiling 45,500ft (13,720m), (Mk 2) 42,000ft (12,800m), (Mk 5) 45,800ft (13,960m).
Number built:	(Exc. prototypes and pre-production aircraft) 126 (20 Mk 1s, 16 Mk 2s, 90 Mk 5s). In addition, 25 Mk 3s, 8 Mk 4s, 1 Mk 6 and 14 Mk 7s were produced.

It quickly became clear that, with its acceleration in reheat, and rapid deceleration using its huge 'barn-door' flap-cum-air-brake, the Swift could give a spectacular display for the initiated and layman alike. Flight Lieutenant Lou Cockerill was quick to spot these virtues and put them to good use in a fine display at RAF Swinderby on Battle of Britain Day in 1956. It is worth repeating, verbatim, a report on the F.R.5's appearance there in the *Lincolnshire Echo*, because it would be the first of many of its sort:

'Crashing through the air at 710 miles per hour, a sleek, blunt-nosed Supermarine Swift brought 7,000 Swinderby visitors excitedly to their feet on Saturday. It took to the air on a last minute decision, to put up the absolute best in aerobatics, and ended a fantastic aerial display by creasing the edge of the sound barrier. Flight Lieutenant Lou Cockerill got the "go-ahead" and raced out to his machine. Her super-charger roared into life and, with a wave from the cockpit, he hurled the Swift high up into the clouds. 7,000 voices gasped in admiration. Up, up, up he went, roaring like some futuristic rocket. Seconds later the Swift appeared from the direction of Newark completing a series of lightning rolls, arriving overhead before the sound of his plane. After a slow roll and a few loops the Control Tower

COURTESY PHILIP JARRETT

COURTESY RICHARD L. WARD

Above: Swift F.R.5 XD920/'E' in service with No II (AC) Squadron, based at Jever in RAF Germany. It is fitted with the 220-gallon ventral tank. Below: The No II (AC) flight line at Jever. The Squadron had taken delivery of its new aircraft while based at Geilenkirchen in February 1956 but it moved to Jever in October 1957.

announced that the Swift was coming in for "a very fast run", having promised not to smash the sound barrier. He came in low over the field. All eyes were on the streamlined fuselage hurtling towards the station buildings and then in a flash he was overhead. As the roar of rushing air reached the ground the Swift was gone, darting upwards back into the clouds. A breathtaking, magnificent performance, which earned Cockerill and the Swift the applause of the crowd.'

Lou may have stretched his luck a little at Swinderby, and this was certainly the case when he attempted to plant a sonic boom on RAF Gütersloh, perhaps to remind the base that the Swift had really

arrived. Planting sonic booms accurately is an inexact art, and on this occasion Lou succeeded only in disturbing the peace at the nearby headquarters at No 2 Group, RAF Sundern—with some very unwelcome repercussions. Transonic flight overland in Britain and over the Continent would soon be banned, with dire consequences promised for any transgressions.

Gradually the groundcrew got on top of this difficult aircraft and, by February 1957, No 79 Squadron was achieving monthly averages of 250 hours' flying. The pilots of both squadrons were very pleased with the performance of their new mount in their operational training, quickly mastering the use of the F.R.5's Vinten cameras in low-level, high-speed photography. It says much for the men and their machines that, in April 1957, Flight Lieutenants Denis Laurence of No 79 Squadron and Tony Winship of No II Squadron came first and second, respectively, in their class in NATO's international 'Royal Flush' reconnaissance competition.

Air-to-air and air-to ground gunnery were now firmly on the training agenda, and at their first Armament Practice Camp at RAF Sylt in September 1957 No II Squadron scored an overall average of 16.7 per cent against 'flags' towed by Tempests and Meteors at heights between 5,000 and 10,000 feet; in their second APC they raised this average to 22.9 per cent. Achieving these scores had not been easy, but Flight Lieutenant Peter Terry, a flight commander and Pilot Attack Instructor (PAI) on No 79 Squadron, had overcome the difficult problem of harmonising the guns without definitive guidance, after the first round fired on the gun butts to this end not only missed the target but also the 60-foot wall behind! This training should not suggest that the Swifts would have been employed in the fighter rôle in war: only *in extremis* and in self-defence would the F.R.5 pilots expect to take the offensive against the MiG fighters they would face.

The Swift F.R.5 also proved to be an excellent air-to-ground gun platform and, by 1959, scores of 40 per cent were by no means uncommon. However, as with air-to-air, the pilots continued to hone their skills against ground targets simply to be ready to do so in war if tasked, or given clearance to attack any specific target of opportunity on the ground (typically a mobile nuclear missile site), otherwise using their cannon solely to 'keep their enemy's heads down'. Above all, their priority was to gather information on the enemy and return safely with it; they had to resist any temptation to take any offensive action other than in those exceptional circumstances.

Throughout its service in Germany, the F.R.5 continued to be plagued by all manner of unserviceabilities, a point highlighted in a Director of Flight Safety Review of 1958. While pilot-error accidents were below the average for this type of aircraft, those attributed to technical and engineering factors abounded, the rate being twice that of the Hunter, with engine, hydraulic and undercarriage problems predominating. Improvements in this area were slow, but in October 1958 No II Squadron flew 276 hours by day and 23 hours by night (the latter to maintain proficiency should the pilots be required to launch before dawn or land after dark).

It had long been intended to replace the Swifts with Hunter Mk 10s on the two FR squadrons in Germany, and the planned transition began early in 1961. Airworthy Swifts were flown back to Britain, where they were used at technical training schools, on burning areas to train fire crews or merely sold for scrap. Those which were unable to make the flight were simply 'chopped up' ignominiously, perhaps with some pleasure by the more sadistic of the aircraft's groundcrew who had cared for them in their better days.

The pilots had mixed feelings, too. The Swift had come to them under a cloud of suspicion and they had some misgivings as to its suitability in the rôle, but the aircraft had proved all the sceptics wrong. It is no exaggeration to say that in the business of armed reconnaissance it had excelled, routinely beating all-comers in many national and NATO reconnaissance competitions; it could be a powerful weapon against targets on the ground; and, in the right hands, it could defend itself well in its natural habitat at low level. The F.R.5 pilots soon learned how to get the best out of their aircraft, and how to cope with the relatively few routine problems it gave them in the air. In many cases, when critical situations or malfunctions did occur, they found it possible to recover this robust and resilient aircraft safely to base. If any doubts remained as to whether the Swift had sufficient manœuvrability to do the job, these were repeatedly dispelled by spectacular VIP and public displays of the aircraft's true potential. The Swift F.R.5 was indeed 'fit for purpose'.

Right: A four-ship formation of Swift F.R.5s from No 79 Squadron, showing the type's unique wing shape to advantage. XD913 has PRU Blue undersurfaces whereas the others wear High Speed Silver. Notice that, on FR Swifts, the uppersurface camouflage was generously 'wrapped around' the leading edges of the horizontal flying surfaces.

COURTESY PHILIP JARRETT

FROM THE COCKPIT

Group Captain Nigel Walpole OBE BA

IN the mid-1950s, the conventional wisdom had it that the two specialist FR squadrons in RAF Germany operating the allegedly 'fearsome' Swift—flying alone, at low level and without aids, in the demanding, fighter-reconnaissance rôle—would require selected, second-tour pilots. Later, it was even suggested that these pilots should also have had fast-jet experience or, at least, have been put through a course on fast jets before joining the front line.

In fact, I met these criteria when I joined No 79 Squadron in September 1957, having completed my first tour on Hunter F.4s at RAF Oldenburg, with the added advantage of having operated in Germany, albeit in the very different rôle of high-level air defence. At that time, the front-line squadrons in Germany were given a great deal of discretion regarding how they trained their pilots, and on No 79 Squadron the conversion to the Swift F.R.5, and familiarisation with FR itself, depended on previous background and flying experience. In my case the programme was short, to the point and quite adequate. For me there was no formal ground school, merely a number of one-on-one discussions with the Squadron's Qualified Flying Instructor (QFI), armed solely with simple charts of the aircraft's systems and a splendidly brief and concise Pilot's Notes, which

COURTESY PHILIP JARRETT

documented all a pilot needed to know and included an in-flight emergency check list. The 100 pages of this thin booklet, which measured five inches by eight inches, fitted neatly into a flying-suit pocket, and was thus readily accessible. Supervised familiarisation with the aircraft's controls, switches, warning indicators and instrumentation was carried out in a cockpit mock-up, and this whole process took less than three days, before a written test covered all aspects of the aircraft, its operation and possible emergencies.

As a result, I was quite comfortable with the prospect of my first flight in the F.R.5. There being no dual Swift, all F.R.5 flying was solo, and the RAF did not consider it necessary to have a 'chase' aircraft, USAF style. Type conversion for all new pilots arriving on No 79 Squadron without previous fast-jet experience was a little more comprehensive, and in all cases there was the usual work to be done in the circuit, in both power and manual control, some upper air work to show the aircraft's lack of combat capability at height, and a great emphasis on the F.R.5's handling in its natural habitat at low level.

On the day of my first flight, the 'walk-around', cockpit procedures, start-up and after-start checks were supervised by my flight commander, particular attention being paid to the correct selection of aileron and elevator power controls, indicated by two green lights, and to ensure that the trimmers were operative and set as required. On all first sorties, a squadron supervisor would then drive out to the runway threshold to ensure that the newcomer had selected reheat with the brake boost 'on' (3,000 pounds of hydraulic pressure to the main wheel brakes), that ignition had taken place and that the 'eyelids' had opened fully to give maximum thrust on take-off. When he was satisfied, with a 'thumbs-

Left: The Mk 5 head-on. The wide-track undercarriage of the Swift, typical of second-generation jet aircraft, aided stability in landing but in later years would have to be re-thought for new designs when the carriage of under-wing weaponry and drop tanks became *de rigueur* for combat aircraft. Below: 'Your carriage awaits, sir': two members of the vital groundcrew pose with their charge. This Mk 5, which exhibits some well-worn wing leading edges, is fitted with the 220-gallon ventral drop tank, which extended the aircraft's range but compromised its flying qualities to a degree. By the time this mark came into service, the metal-framed cockpit canopy had given way to a totally clear hood, considerably improving the pilot's all-round view from his 'office'—a particularly important aspect of his reconnaissance rôle. It can just be discerned, in this photograph, that RAF aircraft operating from Germany were required to carry bilingual warning notices—the translations here appearing in yellow characters adjacent to the originals.

AUTHOR'S COLLECTION

AUTHOR'S COLLECTION

up', and I had checked that the eyelid 'doll's eye' in the cockpit had turned black, with a jet pipe temperature above 600 degrees Centigrade, I could switch off the brake boost and get under way. Only this first sortie was supervised in this manner, correct engine, reheat and eyelid performance invariably being necessary to get the Swift off a 2,000-yard runway.

My first F.R.5 flight was in a 'clean' aircraft (that is, it had no ventral tank), so the acceleration and climb in reheat was spectacular, and I recall reaching 40,000 feet in slightly less than six minutes, However, in the process I had used 1,200 pounds of fuel—almost one-third of that on board. Since I had heard so much about the inadequacies of the aircraft in the upper airspace, the flight held no surprises there. I found aileron, elevator and rudder control to be adequate in all aspects of flight short of the transonic and supersonic regime, the elevator becoming markedly heavier above 0.88M until the variable-incidence was selected to relieve the pressure. The flap-cum-air-brake, cleared for use at any speed, proved to be a great asset, giving a slight but controllable change of trim above 0.9M.

The aircraft's manœuvrability improved immeasurably as I descended into the lower airspace, and accelerated up to the maximum permitted speed of 600 knots in the 'clean' aircraft (585 knots with ventral tank). The aircraft was notably steady and comfortable at this speed, low level being clearly where the F.R.5 belonged. With 900 pounds of fuel remaining, it was nearly time to land, but before doing so I carried out two low approaches in ideal conditions. Breaking into the circuit at 360 knots, I set the flap to 'Landing' and lowered the undercarriage downwind at 250 knots, turned on to the base leg at 200 knots and the final approach at 175 knots, for a threshold speed of 140 knots. I had been briefed on the importance of getting the landing speed right in the 2,000-yard runway—especially in wet/no wind/crosswind conditions—but the Swift settled well at 140 knots as I lowered the nose wheel on touchdown, applied the brakes and eased the stick fully back, with the VI tail set at –9 degrees, to get maximum weight on to the main wheels. This first trip in the Swift had gone like clockwork and entirely as briefed, I was already confident that this was an aircraft I was going to enjoy flying.

Above: A Swift F.R.5 of No 79 Squadron appears in virtual silhouette against a setting sun.
Right: WK303 of the Squadron makes good time in her climb. It took about six minutes for a Swift to reach 40,000 feet—but this consumed almost one-third of the available fuel.

COURTESY PHILIP JARRETT

The remaining nine sorties in the transition programme also went according to plan, to cover every aspect of flight within the F.R.5's capability. Transonic and supersonic flight proved, as with the Hunter, to be practically a non-event. In the transonic speed range, it was possible to feel a slight forward movement on the stick as the aircraft became supersonic, but neither this nor a hint of rudder movement at the same time had any influence on the aircraft's flight path. Aerobatics took up a lot of sky, more than that required for the Hunter, and for the average pilot the following higher entry speeds were recommended: 460 knots for a loop, 480 for a roll off the top, 520 for a vertical roll and 350 knots for a full-aileron roll. Lower speeds were used by the aerobatic 'aces' who were chosen to display the F.R.5.

Stalls in the landing configuration were practised above 20,000 feet, but were not taken beyond the buffet; left rudder had to be applied to counter the asymmetric effect of the nose wheel door as the undercarriage was lowered, with more rudder or aileron applied as required to correct any directional 'wandering' as speed was reduced below 150 knots. If no action was taken at the onset of buffeting, a very high sink rate would occur if speed was reduced below 115 knots. 'G'-stalling was also on the agenda, being relatively innocuous and well marked below 0.85M. However, there was a risk of pitch-up above 0.85M as stick forces reduced with increases in 'g', when 'g' should not be increased beyond the onset of buffet below 25,000 feet. Spinning was prohibited, and was most unlikely to occur accidentally within the F.R.5's normal *modus operandi*. However, spin recovery procedures were fully briefed in the conversion programme, with final advice that the aircraft should be abandoned if recovery were not effective by a minimum of 15,000 feet.

Manual flying was practised throughout the conversion programme. As opposed to the electrical selection, the Swift had mechanical means of selecting power or manual control, which I found to be preferable. It was important that the aileron trim be set at neutral before selecting manual control in the air (ideally at 250 knots or 0.8M above 5,000 feet), or the pilot could be faced with an unnecessarily heavy control load. Thereafter the aircraft could be flown up to 0.9M or 500 knots in manual, but with increasingly heavy loads as speeds increased. Heavy forces on the elevator could be relieved with use of the trimmer and VI tail. Once I got used to the heavy loads, I found landing in manual safe but uncomfortable, although increasingly difficult in cross-winds or generally turbulent conditions. The Pilot's Notes recommend that, in such conditions, the ventral tank should be jettisoned.

Again, because of the lack of a dual control Swift, instrument training was carried out with a safety pilot in the station's Meteor T.7 or Vampire T.11, culminating, if required, in a test conducted by an Instrument Rating Examiner (IRE). It seems that my Green Rating, gained on the Vampire during my previous tour on the Hunter, remained valid.

As with the ground instruction, I found the flying syllabus for conversion to the F.R.5 simple and entirely satisfactory for my background. Moreover,

Above: Another quartet of No 79 Squadron aircraft, this photograph demonstrating the efficacy of the disruptive grey/green camouflage that was by this time general throughout the Royal Air Force but particularly relevant to the low-level reconnaissance rôle.

none of the pilots I joined on No 79 had had any difficulty converting to the Swift, or using the F.R.5 most effectively in the FR rôle, despite none of them having flown anything more powerful than the relatively simple Meteor. I therefore concluded that the demanding criteria suggested for their successors were unnecessary. That said, it would have been prudent to select pilots for this rôle who were considered to be particularly adept at low flying and low-level navigation, and who appeared to have the potential to operate in this regime alone, and at extremes of range.

My logbook shows that I completed my conversion syllabus of ten sorties in a total of seven hours, at the end of which I was very ready to begin my operational training in FR.

* * *

All the predictions of the test pilots and the operational pilots from AFDS and 2TAF in Germany—that the Swift F.R.5 would serve well in its new rôle—came good. It soon proved admirably suited to the demands of armed reconnaissance at very high speeds at ultra low level. Moreover, by using the

COURTESY PHILIP JARRETT

aircraft's potential to the maximum, the F.R.5 pilots believed that they stood a good chance of surviving the gauntlet of the seemingly endless proliferation of Warsaw Pact defences in the aircraft's most likely operating area, that between the Inner German Border and Berlin.

There were, however, those on the staff, and even on the front line, who continued to question the range limitations of the aircraft, particularly if there was a need to use the reheat repeatedly, and whether it had sufficient manœuvrability at low level. Specifically, could the pilots make best use of terrain-masking, such as would be on offer in the Harz Mountains, evade the MiG fighters, 'jink' on to targets at the last moment and take crucial avoiding action (for example, to avoid heavy concentrations of

Above: A Swift 5 in plan view—purposeful lines, if hardly sleek, and with a wing shape quite unlike any other.
Below and opposite, bottom: Swift F.R.5 XD904, used by Vickers-Armstrong Supermarine for flight trials, in the landing configuration.

COURTESY PHILIP JARRETT

AUTHOR'S COLLECTION

Above: An F.R.5 of No II (AC) Squadron reveals its uppersurface camouflage pattern in a high-speed bank.

flak), especially in the poor visibilities which had to be expected in that part of Germany? The majority of F.R.5 pilots, those who understood the concepts of operation in both NATO and the Warsaw Pact and had first-hand experience, would surely claim that in all these cases the answer was 'yes'. On the matter of range, the Swift was likely to be employed in a target-rich environment, supporting hard-pressed NATO forces in immediate contact with the enemy, well short of Berlin, and in a war which would almost certainly move steadily westwards; longer-range NATO tactical reconnaissance aircraft of the time (the RF-84F, RF-101, RB-66 and Canberra) would deal with target arrays at greater range. All pilots quite rightly wish for more fuel, but with judicious use of the throttle, good speed and careful height management in two very different friendly and hostile airspaces, with allowances made for combat and diversion, the F.R.5s could reach these areas from their two primary bases of Gütersloh and Jever.

COURTESY PHILIP JARRETT

AUTHOR'S COLLECTION

As to manœuvrability, doubters had only to witness the extraordinary low-level aerobatic displays performed by Roy Rimington, Brian Seaman, Roger Pyrah, 'Harv' Harvie and others to convince them that, in the right hands, the Swift had sufficient agility to do the job. Regarding terrain-manœuvring specifically, Dick Green and I proved the point again in F.R.5s in competition against RF-84Fs and RF-101s during NATO's 1958 'Royal Flush' Competition: we were the only pilots able to fly down a narrow, winding valley in the Sauerland, below low cloud covering the tops of each side, to find and report on the targets assigned. Likewise, if flown to its full potential, the Swift could be very effective in evading the attention of contemporary Warsaw Pact (WP) fighters, in turning hard on to a target or in taking crucial avoiding action.

The revolutionary strip-aperture F.95 camera, with a focal length of four or twelve inches, a 70mm format, cycling at four or eight frames a second and

AUTHOR'S COLLECTION

Left, upper: Swift turn-round—refuelling and rearming a No 79 Squadron F.R.5. As can be seen, raising the leading-edge inboard wing panels gave easy access to the Aden's ammunition belts.
Left, lower: Fast and low and just above the treetops—in the tactical reconnaissance rôle, the Swift finally found its true *métier*.
Right: Even faster, even lower. Enemy missiles would have had little chance of catching the Swift, but 'triple-A' and small-arms fire were a concern for the pilots.

AUTHOR'S COLLECTION

with a total of 500 exposures, came in for particularly high praise. Set in three oblique stations, port, starboard and nose-facing, they could provide full cover and acceptable definition at speeds in excess of 500 knots, at heights as low as fifty feet—in an overall performance unprecedented at the time.

Many ex-MiG pilots of that era, interviewed by the author since the end of the Cold War, admitted that had the F.R.5 pilots adopted the operating profiles intended, based on speeds of 500–600 knots at ultra low level, they would have had little to fear from the predominantly gun-armed MiG-15s and MiG-17s that filled the skies over the DDR at that time. While the Soviet and newly formed East German *Nationale Volksarmee* manned a comprehensive radar and communications network, their equipment could not locate targets at the heights at which the Swifts would fly. There was a suggestion that observers, positioned at strategic points on expected penetration lanes, were well rehearsed in feeding raid information into the early-warning system, using simple communications, thereby enabling fighters to position accordingly to carry out visual interceptions. If so, a fighter would have to be in a near-perfect position for an essentially rear-hemisphere attack in order to achieve a 'kill' against such a high-speed target 'jinking in the weeds'. Again because of their flight profile, the Swift pilots did not consider contemporary surface-to-air missiles, or air-to-air missiles, to be a threat

The standard NATO 'low and fast' approach did not, however, offer immunity from small-arms fire from the ground or from dedicated anti-aircraft artillery, which the Warsaw Pact had deployed in huge numbers throughout the DDR, and this was the greatest threat to the F.R.5s. Fixed sites, most of which should have been known to NATO, could be avoided, but mobile units could be found anywhere, only the surprise afforded by the low- and fast-flying aircraft, and last-second avoiding action, then helping survivability. As a last resort, the Swift pilot did have the option of distracting the opposition with fire from his two cannon, an option that most other tactical reconnaissance pilots did not have.

On balance, however, the odds were on the F.R.5 pilots' being able to do the job prescribed and return safely to Allied airspace with much-needed tactical information. In the Swift they indeed had 'the right stuff'.

* * *

As a general rule I was against academic competition between front-line squadrons in the Cold War, in that many were practised for, and flown, in ways that were contrary to the imperatives of proper operational training. However, I readily agree that, if structured correctly, some could have contributed to our collective preparation for war in the deterrent rôle, and indeed I took part in one competition in 1958, with a Swift F.R.5 of No 79 Squadron, that I consider came within that category. It was at the US Air Force base at Spangdahlem, in central Germany, that NATO's tactical reconnaissance squadrons came together to battle it out for a number of trophies—their professional pride, of course, being at stake. For the overall prize, the Grünther Trophy, the competitors were grouped under their respective operational commands, with the Second Allied Tactical Air Force (2ATAF) at that time comprising the British, Belgian and Dutch air forces, competing against 4ATAF, involving the Americans and the French. Below that accolades were awarded to the winning pilots or crews in each class (Day/Night, Long/Short-Range, High/Low-Level).

Well before the main competition, each tac recce squadron and wing flew a series of eliminating rounds to select their national representatives for the ATAF teams, each of which then met independently for short dress rehearsals before deploying to Spangdahlem. I had the good fortune to be selected from No 79 Squadron to fly against the II Squadron team, and then to be one of the three pilots to go forward to the five-day 2ATAF work-up at RAF Wildenrath, which was based as closely as possible on the rules and procedures for 'Royal Flush' that year. The other pilots were Dick Green and Oelof Bergh, both from II Squadron. Finally, it was decided that Dick and I should form the Swift team for the Day, Short-Range class, with Oelof travelling as the reserve, and we were joined by two Canberra crews and a reserve from the squadrons in Germany, to take part in the long-range and night classes.

This team assembled at Spangdahlem on the Sunday afternoon before three days of competition flying, one member of the Swift team having been given clearance to announce his arrival with a 'low pass' over the airfield. It was quite incidental that he targeted the Officers' Club for what he explained later was a final practice run, using the Swift squadron's operational tactic of (very) fast and low (in reheat of course), being quite unaware that this was the venue for an official 'meet and greet' for the competition participants. The Royal Air Force had arrived.

The Day, Short-Range class comprised the Swifts and the Belgian and Dutch RF-84F Thunderflashes of 2ATAF, flying against American RF-84Fs and RF-101 Voodoos, and the French RF-84Fs. I believe the very formidable Voodoos were participating for the first time but cannot recall whether the French were 'players' or 'guests' at this 'Royal Flush'.

Regardless of the aircraft type, the Day, Short-Range competition required each of the pilots to fly three 'missions', over the same targets within the same time frame (and, it was hoped, experiencing the same weather), all within the range of the aircraft with the shortest 'legs' (the Swift). The targets were representative of those which were within NATO's War Plans at the time, those considered 'static' being, typically, bridges, military installations and electronic facilities, and those deemed 'mobile' including troops in the field, a bridging party and a road convoy under way. The mobile targets were provided by military units from all participating nations, which would provide information to the competition referees on their composition, in numbers and type of equipment, on whether they would be camouflaged or partly hidden, and on their accurate positions if they were encamped or their projected positions at particular times of each day if they were on the move. In addition, every target would have an on-site 'umpire' nominated to record the times at which each aircraft type passed overhead or close by and to ensure that they carried out only one pass, did not turn in the area for a longer look, and appeared to be at roughly the correct height and speed. If I remember rightly, the players had to fly between 500 and 1,000 feet, at a minimum of 300 knots—figures far removed from the operational heights and speeds at which the FR Swift pilots trained and would expect to operate in the target area in war (50–100 feet at 500–600 knots).

At that time, these missions were flown 'against the clock', timed from the issue of the task, with briefing material for each target, to the final presentation of Mission Reports and photographs. This postulated the need for NATO tac recce forces to react rapidly and effectively to immediate requests from ground or air forces, for near 'real time' information in the fast-moving battles to be expected should the Cold War turn 'hot'.

This was not simply a test of pilots' abilities and aircraft's capabilities, because it involved whole tac recce teams—albeit microcosms of each reconnaissance force. In addition to the pilots it brought in the target-plotting and briefing teams, including army Ground Liaison Officers (GLO) and Photographic Interpreters (PI); the maintenance men who serviced the aircraft and the rôle equipment (specifically the cameras); and the Mobile Field Processing Units (MFPU). All were essential to the successful prosecution of the mission. This was very much a team effort, with each member very dependent on the others—as my story here will show.

At the start of the first flying day, the early-morning weather check reported that conditions

Right: Plenty of Norwegian geology and residual snow but rather less evidence of No II (AC) Squadron's WK300 in this F.95 camera shot. The environment is a far cry from that originally envisaged when the Swift was first mooted.

COURTESY ROY RIMINGTON

AUTHOR'S COLLECTION

around Spangdahlem and in the target areas were acceptable, with wisps of mist hanging in the Eifel valleys that were forecast to burn off and skies otherwise cloudy to partly cloudy, with a general base of 1,500 feet. Dick Green was the first Swift pilot get airborne and I followed on the second wave. I and a USAF Voodoo pilot were handed our tasking material together and the race was on. I took a quick look at my three targets: a small airfield in the Hunsrück, a bridge north of Darmstadt and a 'military unit', encamped and camouflaged in a wooded area on the edge of Baumholder range, looked reasonably simple, all being near good feature lines.

With very little route-planning or map-preparation required, I was running to my Swift within minutes, while the GLOs plotted the initial points I had chosen and the exact co-ordinates of each target on 1:50,000 maps, before folding them as they knew I liked them. By the time the maps were rushed to me I had strapped in, started the engine with the F.R.5's excellent cartridge system and was ready to move out of the revetted pan for a competition priority take-off. Normally, we ran the engine up and engaged reheat with the brake boost selected 'on', to check that all was well before we 'rolled', but by this time I had sufficient confidence in the aircraft to 'plug in the burner' as I rounded on to the long runway, saving precious seconds—and all was well. 'Cleaning up' the aircraft and coming out of reheat as I set up a rough heading for the first target, I flew at 500 knots plus to a nearby feature line, and adjusted my heading to overfly the first IP for the airfield target, reducing speed to 360 knots, selecting and checking the port-facing camera to cycle at eight frames a second for a run 'down-sun'. There being no activity at this private airfield, my simple visual report would consist of an aircraft count, an assessment of the grass runway dimensions, a description of hangars and facilities and comments on access and security, noting all this on my kneepad in my personal brand of shorthand.

As I left this target, I gave a 'clearing burst' on my port camera and sped towards the second at maximum (dry) throttle, on another rough heading, again finding it easily, and noting a 'through-type', steel girder truss road bridge, with masonry piers and concrete abutments, and used the port camera again to minimise the work to follow in the MFPU. The third target presented a challenge. Would the troops be where they were reported to be, hidden too deeply in the woods and be well camouflaged? And would they 'freeze' when they heard my aircraft inbound, to deny me tell-tale movement? Again I was lucky: well before this target, at the regulation minimum of 500 feet, I noticed a wisp of smoke above the trees, and then a whip aerial from a radio van silhouetted against the skyline, close to the position given. This gave me an exact location, and although I could see little in between the trees I was able to identify a Belgian armoured unit—and my port camera revealed a great deal more detail to the well-trained PI.

With time now of the essence, and fuel available, I headed back to Spangdahlem at low level in reheat, adding notes to my kneepad as I did so. Breaking into the circuit at 500 knots, I landed, turned off short on 'Spang''s long runway and taxied in rather faster than I should to get the port camera offloaded and rushed to the MFPU. All the information, plus the prints, was handed to the umpire within thirty minutes of 'engine off'.

Incidentally, I see from the entry in my logbook for that sortie, on 8 September 1958, that I was airborne for just forty minutes, and I recall that, as I taxied in, the Voodoo pilot, who had been given his task at the same time as I, was just taking off. When

I came to fly with a USAF Voodoo squadron later, I understood why it took rather longer for them to get airborne. For me, the day had gone well: everything had worked like clockwork, in a true team effort. But it was not always so.

On day two, the weather was distinctly marginal, but in the way of the day, we were asked to 'give it a go'. One task, given to all pilots in my class at ten-minute intervals, involved a route reconnaissance of a winding road running north-to-south down a Sauerland river valley, in which a German infantry convoy was reported to be wending its way south. All the pilots competing reported, correctly, that, within the allotted time window, cloud was covering the tops of the hills either side of the valley, the Voodoo and Thunderflash pilots aborting that target. My later experience with both these aircraft soon persuaded me that they had been very wise to do so: neither had the manœuvrability to follow that route below the prevailing cloud base. However, with judicious use of the Swift's reheat, and its huge flap and air brake, Dick Green and I were able to enter the valley at northern mouth and follow it most of the way before prudence advised us to pull out. Dick found the convoy, as did his cameras, and he received the highest marks in our class for this sortie. I failed to find any military activity along the road—which was not surprising because the route which had been plotted for me, although parallel and very similar, was several miles to the east. While the Swifts did not win in their class in this 'Royal Flush', as they had in the previous year and would do so in the next, they did contribute markedly to another victory for 2ATAF in the Grünther Trophy. In the late 1950s the Supermarine Swift F.R.5 was a winner all round.

Opposite page: Ground engine runs are not easy on the ears, and reheated engine runs are visually impressive too—especially in the dark. Here a Swift F.R.5 demonstrates.

Below: Sortie over, the pilot departs for his briefing while support crewmen extract the Vinten F.95 camera magazines so that the film can be processed. These were the days, of course, before satellites, drones and 'real-time' imagery revolutionised the task of aerial reconnaissance.

Apart from the unrealistic speeds and heights, and lack of in-flight reporting facilities at that time, I considered this concept of this competition to be acceptable. Throughout the eliminating rounds, every pilot on the tactical reconnaissance squadrons had the opportunity to show his mettle and to represent his squadron, nation and ATAF in 'Royal Flush'. Most importantly, all the competitors within their respective classes were judged on their coverage (or otherwise!) of the same targets, in roughly the same time frame and weather, and so there was a fair comparison of skills.

This is no place to delve further into the pros and cons of academic reconnaissance competitions; suffice it to say that I deplored the lack of operational realism—the basis for direct comparison between

AUTHOR'S COLLECTION

Above: Accidents involving Swift pilots occurred from time to time, for example when Flight Lieutenant (now Air Commodore) Bob Barcilon experienced an undercarriage malfunction and landed on starboard main gear and nosewheel only while on detachment in France in the winter of 1960, ending up 'in a foreign field' (Grostenquin).

units—and the 'gamesmanship' that developed over the years, and also the amount of time spent by some NATO squadrons in training for them with such non-operational practices. Be that as it may, the Swift F.R.5 had all the necessary attributes to excel in the rôle, on whatever terms, and did so with unfailing regularity. Moreover, from the cockpit, the pilots knew it.

* * *

The story of the Swift F.R.5s on the front line in Germany is littered with tales of woe in the air, but many had happy endings, with the survival of all but one of its pilots and many of the aircraft being landed successfully—to fly again. There were very few accidents that could be ascribed to pilot error, the majority being brought about by technical or engineering factors, one of which, attributed to a servicing error, had fatal consequences. In 1957, Flight Lieutenant Greenhalgh, a pilot on detachment from the APC staff at Sylt, lost his life when the canopy of his Swift detached in the air, striking him on the head to render him unconscious.

The first of many mishaps to the F.R.5 fleet in Germany occurred at RAF Gütersloh, on 24 January 1957, when Flight Lieutenant Roger Pyrah was unable to get the port main wheel down for landing. To minimise the risk of fire, he dropped his ventral tank on the airfield golf course, landed on the grass beside Runway 09 and steered his way skilfully among various obstructions for the aircraft to come to rest safely, and with little damage, conveniently close to the maintenance hangar where it was quickly repaired, soon to fly again. Another of No 79's aircraft was not so fortunate: it was damaged beyond repair when two of its starter cartridges ignited simultaneously, sending debris in all directions. In a third incident on the Squadron, Flying Officer Ian Waller lost six feet of wing fillet when recovering from a strafing pass at Nordhorn Range. This caused the aircraft to yaw through 30 degrees at high speed, but Ian had no difficulty recovering it to base.

Flight Lieutenant John Whittam, of No II (AC) Squadron, is believed to have been the first of the F.R.5 pilots in Germany to have had a complete engine failure in the air: in February 1957 he carried out a flame-out controlled descent through cloud, to land skilfully at RAF Wildenrath. Flight Lieutenant Lou Cockerill, of No 79 Squadron, survived another flame-out landing there in May. In further testament to the Swift's strength, both aircraft were repaired to fly again. No II Squadron moved to RAF Jever in the autumn of 1957, and in the very cold winter which followed, it suffered two undercarriage failures, when de-icing sand spread on the paved surfaces jammed the undercarriage locks. Two more undercarriage failures, in 1958, were caused by other defects in the system. In May 1958 a hydraulic failure occurred during a gunnery sortie at Sylt, which necessitated an instrument recovery in manual control, down to a cloud base of 200 feet, and ended with a very difficult crosswind landing, all of which earned Flying Officer Danny Lavender a Green Endorsement in his logbook.

In July 1957 Flight Lieutenant Mike Davis of No 79 Squadron was the first of the front-line pilots to eject from a F.R.5 when, at 800 feet over Hamm, his engine failed. The second was Flight Lieutenant Geoffrey Lee, in May 1958, when he had flight control problems during an air test, but five ejections that were to follow were prompted by engine failures. In every case the pilot survived, albeit with various degrees of injury. Flight Lieutenant Eric Smith was badly hurt after ejecting from a No 79 Squadron F.R.5 west of Hamburg: he parachuted into open countryside and was taken, covered in mud and blood, on a ladder as a stretcher, by German farm workers to a nearby cottage. There, with surprisingly little delay, he was attended by a doctor, who gave him a mighty injection directly into his chest and filled a gaping wound with a noxious yellow powder. When the bill for this treatment arrived, the 'doctor' turned out to be a vet.

It was again at Sylt, in April 1959, that Flight Lieutenant 'Bunny' St Aubyn had one of the most dramatic escapes. His engine failed, accompanied by very severe vibration, over the sea and too far from the island to make a safe landfall. Guided ably by his wingman, Al Martin, he ejected at 3,000 feet, got rid of his oxygen mask and inflated his Mae West, but his automatic separation system failed and he only managed to kick the seat free to hang perilously close some fifteen feet below him as he hit the water. The seat then dragged him down 'to a considerable depth', and when he eventually surfaced he found himself entangled in his parachute shroud lines, preventing him from climbing aboard his dinghy and the winchman from hauling him into the rescue helicopter. It was therefore decided to tow pilot, dinghy and parachute a few feet above the waves to the nearby shore, a journey which, 'Bunny' recalls, left him 'very cold, confused and uncomfortable'; he was also injured with stretch and compression fractures. It transpired that the fracture of a single blade had led to the disintegration of the entire engine compressor—hence the vibration—and that Bunny's oxygen tube had fouled the parachute harness, preventing the seat from separating automatically.

Roger Pyrah and the F.R.5 hit the headlines again in July 1959's edition of *Flight Comment* when he dealt successfully with a fire in the air, caused by a hydraulic leak, just after take-off. With the fire warning light fluttering on and off as smoke and flames spewed from the rear end of his aircraft, the flight controls reverted to manual and Roger was only deterred from ejecting by his proximity to a densely populated area. He continued his recovery, manœuvring the aircraft at low level with great difficulty while the fire warning light continued to blink intermittently, finally to land at Gütersloh. For averting a major disaster on the ground and saving his aircraft, he was rewarded with a well-earned 'Good show!' in his logbook.

In August 1959 Roy Rimington was the second No II Squadron pilot to eject into water, in the rather unusual circumstances of inverted flight over the River Weser at Porta Westfalica, near Minden. Flight Lieutenant 'Taff' Wallis was with him, their aim to get a suitable photograph for the Squadron Christmas card against a background of the 300-foot

Below: On 21 May 1957 XD930's engine flamed out and would not relight, so the pilot, Flight Lieutenant Lou Cockerill, was obliged to make a forced landing at Wildenrath, with the ventral tank—which, it was officially advised, should be jettisoned in such circumstances—still *in situ*. This was the result. Notice the detached cockpit canopy in the right foreground.

AUTHOR'S COLLECTION

COURTESY BOB BARCILON

No II (AC)'s F.R.5 XD972, with ventral tank, speeds over the West German countryside, the pilot's vital reference material handily stowed against the windshield.

statue of Kaiser Wilhelm on the river bank. They got more than they bargained for when, on one of his inverted runs, Roy's engine gave out and refused to relight. He rolled 180 degrees, managed to gain some height and ejected—only to black out. To compound his predicament, his parachute harness malfunctioned and he descended at some velocity, headfirst, into the river, his progress slowed only thanks to the fact that the harness had become entangled round his leg.

In the same month, No II Squadron's charismatic flight commander Oelof Bergh had multiple problems while leading the third pair in a large formation take-off, with many aircraft following behind him. His difficulties began with a hydraulic failure which caused the flight controls to revert to manual and left the undercarriage and flap extended. Continuing the take-off to minimise confusion behind him, he hit the slipstream of the aircraft ahead as he broke away, an uncomfortable experience in manual, at which point the cockpit filled with smoke, the cockpit cold air unit seized and the starboard wing fuel transfer pump failed. It was clearly time to return to the ground, and this Oelof did in exemplary fashion to win another Green Endorsement for the Squadron. Derek Gathercole then added to this tally when he was forced to make another emergency landing in the same aircraft during the subsequent air test. In this case the fuel control unit failed, leaving him with a mere 4,500rpm to recover from 18,000 feet, in what the *Flight Comment* magazine called 'Another splendid example of skill and good airmanship'.

In November 1960 Flight Lieutenant Pat King, No 79 Squadron, tested the Swift's rugged strength to the limit when he flew his F.R.5 through the tops of tall trees while on an operational training sortie in the Sauerland—and brought his aircraft safely back to Gütersloh. The evidence that he had done so was undeniable, the underside of his aircraft remaining decorated with foliage but short of the aerials which were there when he had taken off.

The final ejection within the F.R.5 force took place at Gütersloh in March 1960, Flight Lieutenant John Nevill flaming-out on the break to land on Runway 09. Three attempts to relight the engine downwind failed as his speed bled off alarmingly, with any hope of his completing a safe landing diminishing equally rapidly. He left his ejection until the very last moment, at a height he estimated to be 100 feet (this was later assessed to have been no more than 60 feet), perhaps the lowest of all the Swift ejections; he can have been on the end of his parachute for no more than a couple of seconds before landing in a ploughed field. As with several others who had ejected, John suffered from compression fractures which kept him in hospital for three weeks, but he was off flying for only three months.

In June 1960 it was No II Squadron's Flight Lieutenant Phil Crawshaw's turn to go careering off the runway with one wheel firmly locked up, but he committed the heinous act of cutting across the

COURTESY RICHARD L. WARD

Above: WK313 at rest. There appears to be a rival squadron's 'zap' on the main intake—good-natured byplay not infrequently practised when units flew in to visit one another.
Below: Squadron Leader C. S. MacDonald's Swift F.R.5 XD962, here seen at RAF Biggin Hill for the Battle of Britain Open Day in September 1960—the month 'Mac' MacDonald took over command of No II (AC) Squadron. Another photograph of this aircraft appears on page 69 and a colour photograph taken on the same occasion as that above is seen on page 96, while a more sombre portrait can be seen on page 103.

fourth fairway of the airfield golf course—a crime which cost him 60 pfennigs. When everything calmed down, and the aircraft was jacked up, the offending wheel was persuaded to emerge from the wing and lock down by a well aimed blow from a sledge hammer.

There were still more incidents to come. In January 1961, in what might be called their swan-song, Swifts took part in a big formation of NATO aircraft, of many types, and this time it was Flight Lieutenant Pete Adair of No II Squadron who had to break away immediately after take-off at Brüggen, with severe engine vibration, to drop his ventral tank on the airfield and land back there just as his engine seized. He then became a spectator in a silent cockpit, ignored by all as his hosts dealt with a small fire on the airfield, caused by fuel from the wreck of his ventral tank.

So ends this litany of woes which beset the RAF's Swift F.R.5 force in Germany, and it was now perhaps time for the venerable Swift to be replaced by the Hunter F.R.10, but it is worth repeating that in five years of excellent service only one pilot was killed in a Swift—and this was neither the fault of the pilot nor that of the aircraft.

COURTESY PHILIP JARRETT

Get Swept! *Flight Lieutenant Brian Luffingham*

The Swift was very long overdue and thus anticipation on No 79 Squadron was enormous when the day—14 June 1956—actually arrived. Everyone was out on the pan to see the arrival and taxy in. The FR squadrons were just about the last to receive modern aircraft: by this time the old Meteor was not in keeping with our desired 'image', and other fighter squadrons would regularly tease us and tell us to 'get swept'. That hurt!

The first people to convert to the new jet were the Flight Commanders and the Qualified Flying Instructors (QFIs). The remaining pilots were then given a ground school course on systems etc. and sent off to begin a series of eleven conversion sorties, all of which occupied about three weeks.

The day prior to the beginning of the conversion course I went up in a Meteor 7 with the Flight Commander in order to explore general handling, instrument flying (I/F) and low-flying; my log book then shows the following sequence of events for the completion of conversion to the Swift:

1. General handling.
2. Manual controls (QGH).
3. Manual controls (GCA).
4. Reheat climb (45,000 feet).
5. Manual; aeros; QGH.
6. Supersonic (45,000 feet).
7. High speed/low level .
8. Manual landing; supersonic.
9. Aeros; manual; QGH.
10. General handling.
11. General handling; practice forced landing.

After this we were, at long last, 'swept'!

A couple of stark memories. First, the wire voice recorder fitted to the aircraft proved to be a total waste of space; useless, in fact. It was tried out just the once—and never used again by anybody. Secondly, our gunnery scores were consistently low. On investigation it was found that the manufacturers had fitted one of the weapon's critical components in a ridiculous position as it was subject to massive gun firing vibrations, thereby producing errors.

Owing to its generally poor performance at altitude, the Swift was officially classified 'non-operational above 10,000 feet' (!)—which explains how and why it was assigned to the fighter-reconnaissance (low-level) rôle. Once, on a clear day right above our airfield, and with low fuel/weight, I strived repeatedly, with reheat, to get to 50,000 feet (QNH pressure setting), but, however I tackled it, I just could not make the last 300 feet. The aircraft simply fell out of the sky.

It was, nevertheless, very strongly built—possibly too strongly built. Hitherto, the Meteors were frequently to be seen in the hangar with bird-strike damage, more often than not meaning holes in the leading edges of the wings, and I understand that, in later years, there were often three or four Hunters awaiting their turn for similar repairs. But I never saw a Swift in the hangar with bird-strike damage.

This extra strength had its drawbacks, as it was in part the result of a large number of poor design features incorporated in the Swift—which was, of course, originally designed as a high-altitude interceptor fighter. Some of these features meant that extra weight was needlessly incorporated. As an example, the Meteor, in common with many of its contemporaries, had undercarriage doors that were activated by mechanical interaction with the main undercarriage assembly for opening and closing operations.

COURTESY BRIAN LUFFINGHAM

COURTESY BRIAN LUFFINGHAM

Opposite page, above and below: The first Swift arrives on No 79 Squadron at Wunstorf, 14 June 1956, flown in by ferry pilot Flight Lieutenant Graham Elliott. The belly tank would have been mandatory for the flight from RAF Benson. The aircraft, which will in due course receive squadron markings and a tail code letter–'A', of course–is XD925.

Simple! But the Swift, I seem to remember, had two hydraulic jacks to each main door with all the attendant individual hydraulic pipes, fluids, fittings and so on. It even, rather ridiculously, had two hydraulic jacks for the solitary nosewheel door. Unserviceability of the aircraft was notorious, the difficulties exacerbated by the fact that too many simple problems required the engine to be physically removed in order that maintenance personnel could gain the necessary access for repairs.

It was also discovered that the wings had massive blocks incorporated into their design that were to be utilised for 'picketing/securing' the aircraft to the ground in very windy weather. I never actually saw these blocks within the wings,

COURTESY BRIAN LUFFINGHAM

COURTESY BRIAN LUFFINGHAM

but it was common knowledge that we carried our picketing rings with us if we climbed up to 45,000 feet to do our regular supersonic run practice!

Despite its perversions, however, we all loved the Swift. It was the only aircraft I flew that got better the faster it went—and it was capable of 0.96 Mach (600-plus knots) with reheat on the deck. It was, indeed, the first aircraft in the RAF to have an afterburner. Use of this facility (termed 'wet') required two and a half times more fuel than flying with full power 'dry'. It was a quite wonderful change from the days of the Meteor and Vampire. But there were further problems, since after about a year on the Squadron the aircraft began to experience engine failures.

I had one 'hairy' moment. Once, ready to take off from Sylt, I pressed the 'start' button. In the Swift, this fired a cartridge that spun the starter motor to 60,000rpm, but the motor blew up and shattered, its bits blasting holes throughout the aircraft and totally destroying my 'Sugar' (XD954). The worst part was my last split-second vision of the outside world before everything was enveloped in smoke. Everyone was running away from the aircraft . . . and I had yet to undo four seat straps, four parachute straps, the G-suit, the radio plug, the dinghy connection and two oxygen connections and then slide the canopy back before I could even start to climb out into the invisible outside world! The aircraft was written off.

COURTESY BRIAN LUFFINGHAM

Above and left: Some glimpses into No 79 Squadron's accommodation at Wunstorf. In the photograph above, the Swift on the left has its camera ports shuttered off in order to protect the glazing. In flight, these shutters could be operated manually, but they also opened automatically when the cameras were selected by the pilot. The glazing in the nose was peculiarly vulnerable to impact with insects and to general erosion, of course. Right: Flight Lieutenant Denis Laurence in No 79 Squadron's WK295 flashes past the *Hermannsdenkmal* in Lippe, West Germany—a landmark familiar to RAF aircrew and known to all generally (but not exclusively) as 'Hermann the German'. The statue commemorates the tribal chieftain whose warriors defeated a Roman army in A.D. 9.

COURTESY BRIAN LUFFINGHAM

No Instant Response *Squadron Leader Bob Broad*

In the 1950s the RAF had the Central Fighter Establishment (CFE) to advise on fighter tactics, aircraft and training. I had always assumed that this was a fall-out from the Battle of Britain, when no such organisation existed: while we scraped through at that time, we should have done better.

CFE was headed by an Air Commodore (John Grandy in my time) and occupied its own airfield, RAF West Raynham. It consisted of:

1. An Operations section, headed by a Group Captain, which acted as a 'think tank' and organised and controlled the various trials.
2. The Day Fighter Leaders' School (DFLS)—best described as an early 'Top Gun' outfit.
3. The Air Fighting Development Squadron (AFDS), which was the trials squadron for day fighters.
4. The All-Weather Development Squadron (AWDS), which was the trials squadron for night/all-weather fighters.
5. The Instrument Rating Squadron (IRS), which trained Instrument Rating Examiners.

The development process for fighter aircraft in those days was a little convoluted and not very successful. CFE/AFDS were currently quite well regarded as they had correctly identified that the Swift was no good as a day fighter; Boscombe Down (who, to be quite fair, had noted all the problems) had not been as clear-cut in their expressed opinion. When I joined AFDS there was still talk about the CO being rushed off to waiting rooms in Whitehall to brief ministers.

AFDS was then a somewhat unusual squadron headed by a Wing Commander, a Squadron Leader Flight Commander and about seven or eight Flight Lieutenants (including one from the US Air Force and one from the Royal Canadian Air Force). Almost all had been Flight Commanders and were experienced. AFDS also had its own stable of aircraft, which, when I joined, consisted of half a dozen or so Hunters of various marks, a Meteor F.R.9 and a Meteor T.7; a pair of Swift Mk 5s was awaited.

The rôle of AFDS was to undertake trials on any day fighter developments. It had conducted an evaluation of the Swift Mk 1, damning it completely. There was a slight overlap with Boscombe Down, but in theory AFDS got the aircraft as it entered service and 'wrung it out'. It is perhaps pertinent to recall the Venom, which AFDS revealed to have a fragile wing (fatally) and the R/T switches placed so that formation let-downs were dangerous.

However, testing aircraft was only part of the rôle; tactics and equipment were also tried out. AFDS was also a centre of experience: when I was there pilots had flown almost every fighter then in service, including the MiG-15. We were rather expected to be able to fly anything, and when I did go solo in a Swift there was no suggestion of any ground school: I took off merely with a copy of the Pilot's Notes handy. Finally, during the annual air defence exercises (and presumably national emergencies) AFDS and DFLS formed a front-line squadron filled out with pilots from Operations and the IRS. This once gave me the unusual experience of leading a flight with a Group Captain as my Number Two and a Wing Commander as my Number Three.

An officer assigned to AFDS started as a 'new boy' and progressed with time, as people were posted out, and experience to become a project officer on some of the trials. The trials in which I was involved, or for which I eventually became project officer, were:

Hunter with TACAN.
Hunter with radio compass.
Development of standard let-down for Hunter and other fast jets.
Evaluation of Mystère 4a (pre-Suez).
Evaluation of Swift F.R.5.
Evaluation of Hunter F.6.
Evaluation of Hawker P.1109 (i.e., 'Hunter night fighter').
Checking V-bomber with anti-flash paint visibility (visible at 80 miles).
Hunter v. Canberra trials.
'BABS 4' trial.
'Rebecca 8' trial.
Hunter electric tail.
Hunter extended leading edge.
Hunter with 24 R/P.
Hunter with 2 × 1,000-pound bombs.
New oxygen regulator trial. (This represented AFDS at its best. Testing an oxygen regulator in a single-seat aircraft is actually very risky—rather more risky, in fact, than we appreciated. We were given six regulators to test; they were installed in our aircraft and normal flying was carried out. Two failed on me and one—I believe—failed on a Swift. At that point they were summarily sent back to the manufacturer.)
Partial pressure helmet trials.

When the Swift Mk 5 arrived at AFDS I was still very much a 'new boy' and did not get involved in the trial immediately. One of our two Swifts went thoroughly u/s, which meant that Swift flying time was scarce, and so they concentrated on the FR side of its capabilities. I thought at the time that we should investigate its air combat abilities, but pressure of flying hours meant that this area was very much on the back-burner. However, on one occasion—and I cannot recall how it came about although I think it must have been at the end of our sorties—I was flying a Hunter 4 on some trial (probably checking let-down settings) and Alan Woodcock (the AFDS Flight Commander) was in the Swift. We met up and went to check the turning powers of the Swift. I was on the Swift's tail at about, I suppose, 200 yards and called for a break. The Swift had a good and effective tail, arguably better than that of the early Hunters, and what we thought would happen would be that the

Right: A photograph of a low-flying No 79 Squadron Swift F.R.5 taken by its companion via the port F.95 camera; notice that the subject aircraft has its starboard camera position closed off. The shadows of both aircraft are cast below.

COURTESY BOB BARCILON

Above: A 'tail-chase' view of a Swift F.R.5 of No II (AC) Squadron on a reconnaissance exercise over Germany. It was at these sorts of altitudes, rather than at tens of thousands of feet on interceptor duties, that the Swift proved to be an valuable asset.

Swift would get into its turn more quickly and then the Hunter would catch up; then reheat could be tried.

What actually happened shook me. The Swift indeed went into its turn quickly, as we had anticipated, and its plan view came into sight, but it did not get out of my flight path and I had to work quickly to avoid it.

That was it. I cannot recall if someone else checked it: I think we just realised that agility was not the Swift's strong point and let it pass. What, due to my inexperience, I failed to realise was that Supermarine's claim that the Swift was ideal for FR had some real justification. (Frankly, we thought that they would have claimed it was ideal as an anti-submarine aircraft if they thought that this would sell it!) However, a lack of instant response to an incidence change is bad for air combat but great for gusts at high speed and low level.

I actually went on to fly some ten hours in the Swift, mostly flying profiles to check its range. AFDS was very careful about making sure that if they said that an aeroplane could do a particular profile, then we had checked it.

COURTESY BRIAN LUFFINGHAM

Sixth Sense *Squadron Leader Phil Crawshaw MBE*

My training for the specialities of the fighter-recce rôle took place at Chivenor, where FR trainees progressed from the Hunter to an FR training detachment, three or four of us at a time being instructed in the necessary requirements of the task. There was a qualification in that all participating in the course had to have completed at least one operational tour—there were no 'first-tourists'. Flight profiles were practised with an instructor in a Hunter T.7, and from there I moved back to a single-seat Hunter, flying sorties with the instructor following in a chase aircraft to determine that photographic targets were being correctly located and approached. The training course lasted for some six weeks, and at the finish I was posted to No II Squadron at Jever to fly the Swift, where, after a couple of weeks making holes in the sky and generally getting a feel for the aircraft, the work of fighter-reconnaissance began in earnest. On the Squadron there were a Training Flight Commander and an Operational Flight Commander, and the former would devise a number of training sorties that new pilots would be required to complete successfully before they could be declared operational. This phase entailed some eight or ten Swift sorties a week and lasted about six weeks, after which 'war targets' could be tackled with the more experienced members of the Squadron.

In the Swift FR rôle, we used a very simple system for navigation. Each pilot had a map with a sheet clear film fixed over it, and the briefed route would be marked in using a chinagraph pencil, together with the heading. Care would be taken to note the presence of any high-tension cables—a serious hazard for low-fliers! The route would be subdivided into 30-second or one-minute intervals (depending on the mileage involved). A prominent feature close to the target would be selected from the map to serve as a 'waypoint', and the target would be defined, and flown, from that position. Thus it could be established at the beginning whether the target would appear on the left-hand or the right-hand side of the aircraft, and whether the forward-looking camera would be required. In practice, the nose camera—referred to as the 'nose-facer'—was utilised much less frequently than the side-facing cameras. It was preferable when conducting a line search, for example when tackling an elongated feature such as a canal with a series of bridges or other crossing points that needed to be photographed, even though the resulting pictures were generally smaller, with perhaps less detail of each individual target and more hinterland in the frames.

As the target proper was approached, the cameras were switched on and made 'live' via the console on the right-hand cockpit sidewall, where camera selection (a choice of using either one or two cameras) and aperture (to a limited extent—between f4 and f8, as I recall) were also selected. The operation of the shutters was facilitated by means of a button on top of the pilot's control stick; shutter speed (1/1,000th or 1/2,000th sec.) was set automatically. Opposite cameras were only rarely employed together, the objective of the recce pilot being to capture an image of the target in as few frames of film as possible (since this made the post-sortie task of 'reading' the film a lot easier). The film was fed through the camera at eight (or, on the Swift, optionally four) frames per second, and every effort was made to ensure that the target was safely recorded in eight to twelve frames. The cameras were fixed, so the alignment of the target had to be undertaken by the pilot, who would manœuvre his Swift into the optimum position, ensuring (if a sideways-looking camera was being utilised) that the target would, as it were, pass down the side of the fuselage. One feature of the Swift was its remarkable reluctance to change direction: at high speed, the aircraft required a stretch of airspace about six miles wide in order to turn 180 degrees, and so it was even more important to hit the target first time. Accurate alignment in the final run-in could be assisted by using the aircraft itself (for example, the wing) as a sort of datum, but of course the best teacher for skilled photographic reconnaissance was experience: after a while, pilots developed a kind of sixth sense and were able to capture well-centred images as a matter of routine.

On landing back at base, the film was removed from the aircraft, whistled into the Photographic Unit (or MFPU, Mobile Field Photographic Unit), developed and dried, typically all in about five minutes. The film was then placed over a light table and the pilot would select the photographs

required for printing—usually two but occasionally three images would be chosen. Some five minutes later, the frames would have been fully processed and prints made available. This work was often carried out in the presence of a Photographic Interpreter, a specialist who would have direct liaison with the unit (generally in the charge of an Army Ground Liaison Officer) that had required the photographic intelligence in the first place. The resulting prints were approximately nine inches square, and the degree of detail, thanks to the qualities of the Vinten F.95 camera, always outstanding.

The debrief for the pilot was a vital part of the sortie. Occasionally a voice recorder would have been used by the pilot and this could play an important part in the debrief (particularly if there had been three or four targets to be photographed in the course of a single sortie), but more often the debrief was simply a oral, face-to-face report, in which the pilot would relay any additional information he might have gleaned about the target, for example, whether it was stationary or moving and whether it was supported by other, more distant enemy forces. Both the photographs and details of the verbal debrief would, as quickly as possible, be passed on to the authority that had requested the information (usually an Army unit).

In a genuinely hostile arena, the Swift pilot would have employed his high speed and his ultra-low altitude as his defences; dealing with enemy fire was not something that he could realistically be trained for, so this aspect of his duties was to a great extent 'by guess and by God'. While training in Germany we were not permitted to fly at less than 250 feet above ground level (AGL); in the event of hostilities, this would have been reduced quite considerably, presenting enemy gunners with an exceptionally difficult tracking problem. The aircraft's reheat was a valuable asset, however: when engaged, it gave the Swift a substantial 'kick' and could help get the pilot out of trouble if he encountered it. Navigation at the exceptionally low altitudes dictated by genuine hostilities would, admittedly, have been more difficult for us than during our routine, day-to-day training, which is why we planned our sorties according to elapsed time rather than to the linear distance involved.

I spent about a year flying Swifts, but by early 1961 the Hunter F.R.10 had arrived on the Squadron and the changeover had begun. In addition to converting to a new aircraft, the Squadron had the task of moving its base from RAF Jever in the north of Germany to RAF Gütersloh. The Hunter was familar to most of the pilots involved and the two aircraft had a similar performance and a similar fit, even including the F.95 cameras. Consequently the move was accomplished smoothly and No II (AC) was declared operational in a remarkably short time.

Below: A pair of Swift F.R.5s over Germany, showing their distinctive No II Squadron markings. Unusually, though not uniquely in the RAF, many F.R.5s—especially those in the 'XD' production run—had their fuselage serial numbers applied with the prefix letters well separated from the three numerals, although the reason for this is uncertain.

COURTESY BOB BARCILON

Close to the Deck *Group Captain B. W. ('Danny') Lavender* OBE AFC

My first association with the Supermarine Swift was in 1950–52 when I was a trainee flight test observer with the Percival Aircraft Company, and when a visit to the Farnborough Air Shows was a 'must'. Mike Lithgow put on fabulous displays in the second pre-production prototype, arriving well before the sonic boom, as did Neville Duke and Bill Bedford in the Hunter. I noticed later that Mike never attempted the thirteen-turn spin after the high speed run, and I thought then that there must be a good reason!

Incidentally, I had a narrow escape at the show in 1952 when the D.H.110 flown by John Derry broke up in a tight turn over the airfield and I saw one engine heading straight for us in the Percival Aircraft hospitality stand. Everyone ducked, but it passed overhead and embedded in the hill just a few hundred yards behind, tragically killing 29 spectators. We mourned the loss of John Derry and his flight test observer Tony Richards, but the accident did not put me off my ambition to become an RAF fighter pilot.

I joined up on a short-service commission a few days after my eighteenth birthday and gained my Wings after training on the first Piston Provost/Vampire course at RAF Ternhill and Oakington, respectively. No 56 Squadron at RAF Waterbeach, commanded by Squadron Leader 'Twinkle' Storey, which was only four miles from Oakington, were flying the Swift F.1 at the time, and we often saw it; we also heard about three ejections from the aircraft in fairly close succession and one or two other accidents, which raised our suspicions about the aircraft. However, my operational conversion was onto the F-86 Sabre at RAF Chivenor, and I then joined No 3 (F) Squadron at Geilenkirchen on the Sabre, later flying the Hawker Hunter F.4 as well.

On 23 February 1956 it was announced over the tannoy system that the first Swift F.R.5 to re-equip No II (AC) Squadron, also based at Geilenkirchen, was about to arrive, and we rushed outside to see the aircraft make an unimpressive pass and a very wide circuit and landing. Many of us went out to meet the ferry pilot, who was clearly none too impressed with the handling characteristics of the aircraft. Soon after that, the Duncan Sandys 'axe' descended and the decision was made that Nos 3 and 234 Squadrons on the Station, as well as many others, were to be disbanded because missiles rather than fixed wing aircraft were the future! While most of my fellow pilots were posted to obscure jobs back in Britain, to my surprise and joy I was posted to No II (AC) Squadron at the age of 22 years—the youngest pilot by far.

On 21 June 1957, I clambered into XD912 for my first solo on the F.R.5, climbed to 45,000 feet and was exhilarated by the performance of the reheated Avon. However, when I took the afterburner out in level flight I could scarcely manage to turn and the speed bled off rapidly, almost to the stall. It was clear that high altitude was not the environment for the Swift! My nine conversion flights were completed by 2 July and then the real low-level reconnaissance missions started in earnest. Although aircraft serviceability was very poor, the F.R.5 at low altitude was superb and, hurtling along close to the deck at 420 to 540 knots, the aircraft handled beautifully, it was as stable as a rock and its side- and nose-mounted F.95 cameras produced excellent results. With no other aids apart from a compass, stopwatch and a map with time marks chinagraphed on it, I managed to achieve some excellent results. I quickly became confident that I could complete a reconnaissance of my pre-briefed wartime targets in East Germany and return safely if tasked; in the War Room, frequent updating on the formidable Warsaw Pact air defences became routine. As far as air-to-air combat was concerned, in afterburner and at low altitude the Swift was quite good at evading by staying very

Below: Another pair of Swifts from No II (AC) Squadron, XD920 (foreground) and XD916, lacking both belly tanks and tail letters.

low and fast, but firing on the flag was quite a challenge, particularly ensuring that there was sufficient angle-off to avoid shooting down the towing aircraft. However, I have scores recorded in my logbook of 75 per cent highest and some at over 40 per cent, though most are in the 20s.

During my time on the Swift we had a number of accidents or incidents. However, I was very happy flying the aircraft and had only two 'moments'. As I was accelerating through 240 knots after take-off one day in 1958, the canopy on the port side lifted up a couple of inches. I immediately ducked, pulled up hard, cancelled reheat and put out a pan call to explain my predicament. After burning off fuel at 170 knots for half an hour, I landed without further incident, but I had to wait in the cockpit for another thirty minutes while the engineers tried to fathom out what had gone wrong. To the best of my knowledge, it was finally decided that there was a 'Murphy' in the engineering manual which could result in the canopy being fitted wrongly. This is probably what had happened to Flight Lieutenant Dick Greenhalgh's aircraft in August 1957, when he was killed shortly after take-off when the canopy detached, striking him on the head and causing him to go down with the aircraft.

The Swift was quite difficult to handle in manual control and I did have quite a challenge at armament practice camp at RAF Sylt in XD929 on 22 May 1958 when I experienced a full hydraulic failure shortly after take-off. While burning off fuel for landing, the weather deteriorated rapidly with low cloud down to 200 feet and a strong crosswind; with communication problems so that no radar guidance was possible but just courses to steer, I was very relieved to get the aircraft back on the ground safely. Aden gun stoppages were also a cause for concern, and on one occasion I was sent back to Sylt with Flight Lieutenant Lou Cockerill to carry out a series of gun-firing trials in 4g and 5.5g orbits, which helped identify the problem in the feed mechanism. Some of these sorties were completed in fifteen minutes because we were scarcely out of 'burner!

My last flight in the Swift was on 3 October 1958 from RAF Jever, when I departed Germany bound for the Flying Instructors' School at RAF Little Rissington after two thrilling tours on Nos 3 (F) and II (AC) Squadrons, with 'above average' assessments from both Squadron Commanders, and in love with the Sabre, Hunter, Swift and a BFES school teacher fiancée. My fighter pilot days did not end there—but that is another story!

COURTESY DANNY LAVENDER

Above: Flying Officer (as he then was) Danny Lavender exits his Swift. In contrast to the Swift F.1 and F.2, pilot entry and egress on the Mk 5 was via the port side of the cockpit.

COURTESY PHILIP JARRETT

Below: XD916 again, in clearer focus, captured by the port-facing F.95 camera of its squadron-mate. The paintwork is comparatively fresh.

COURTESY DANNY LAVENDER

The Well-Built Swift *Air Commodore Pat King CBE*

I have good reason to remember the Swift F.R.5, in particular the manufacturer Supermarine, because of the extraordinarily solidly built airframe which I firmly believe saved my skin during an accident that was entirely of my own making. I was at RAF Gütersloh on No 79 (Fighter Reconnaissance) Squadron, which had a low-level Cold War reconnaissance (recce) rôle principally focusing on identifying elements of any Warsaw Pact ground forces. Our training was very demanding in terms of low-level, high-speed navigation in an era when the main navigational tools were a map, a stopwatch and a very high degree of situational awareness, especially on navigational aspects—the aspect I left behind on take-off along with discipline and common sense.

As part of the low-level training, on selected days all pilots flew the same sortie profile, called Exercise 'Poker', and therefore all 'recce'd' the same targets, thus promoting a competitive spirit conducive to high operational standards. In the exercise, points, based mainly on time criteria, were deducted for certain aspects of the whole sortie, beginning with planning.

When you entered the planning room, the officer managing the sortie—let's call him the Planning Manager—handed you a sealed envelope with sortie-specific information and maps of two different scales. The smaller-scale map was for flying your main route up to and including a specific point, known as the Initial Point (IP), for each target. On this map you marked the heading, and, to check progress along track, marks were also normally made at one-minute intervals. The larger-scale map, giving considerably more detail, was for flying from the IP to the target. On this larger-scale map you would mark heading and also, at ten-second intervals, marks along the track from the IP to help you know when you were nearing the target (which sometimes was very difficult to spot).

Planning was timed and had to be completed in less than fifteen minutes. This may sound generous but it was not, given the complex of issues and decisions to be made; and, if the IP to target maps for the four different targets required to be stuck together, that could add considerably to planning your workload. If you took longer than fifteen minutes to complete your planning, points were deducted. If you left the planning room before the time penalty was invoked, but had not completed your planning, you were only adding to the already demanding airborne workload.

In addition to the sortie debrief and considerations of the actual photography, points were deducted for exceeding the time limit set for the duration of the sortie. Timing started from release the brakes until returning to overhead base at circuit height. The height to fly was at 250 feet AGL in authorised low-flying areas, and at other heights outside them. The minimum average speed set for the sortie would be 420 knots. However, to avoid invoking the overall timing penalty, most pilots would fly at about 480 knots so as to have a time margin in order to deal with the unexpected, like bad weather, en route. Moreover, as the timing started at the beginning—the take-off roll—additional speed was needed to offset the time to accelerate to the minimum of 420 knots. As a general practice, any increase in speed was carried out in multiples of 60 knots, each of which equated to a minute (thus 420 knots would be seven miles a minute, 480 knots eight miles a minute, etc.). Using these multiples made airborne (mental) adjustments to timing much easier. On debrief, no excuse or reason whatsoever was accepted for flying at an average speed of less than 420 knots.

Left: The spectacular qualities of the Vinten F.95 and the adroitness of the Swift pilots in capturing their images are borne out by this much-enlarged segment—only a segment—of a frame gathered from the port-facing camera during a recce exercise over Germany.
Below: One of No 79 Squadron's Swift F.R.5s seen fast and low during a sortie from RAF Gütersloh in the late 1950s.

COURTESY BRIAN LUFFINGHAM

COURTESY PAT KING

For safety reasons pilots took off at ten-minute intervals in order to deconflict with other aircraft over the target area. With fierce competition to do well, every effort was made in all aspects of the sortie, starting with planning, to minimise the chance of anyone using excessive initiative—called 'cheating' when done successfully by someone else!—to gain 'unfair' advantage. However, in war who cares if you cheat to win? The attempts of the Poker Manager for the exercise were not invariably successful in limiting excesses of initiative during the planning phase nor during the debrief.

There were four targets planned for my particular sortie and the weather was generally not problematic except for that at the first target, where it was noted as possibly being below the limits authorised in Air Staff Instructions (ASIs). I was to fly the third sortie, taking off ten minutes after the second aircraft. The Squadron Commander, known less formally as 'The Boss', was flying the second sortie, and after I had taken off and changed frequency he reported that the first target was 'weathered out'. I decided to continue because I wished to do well—as we all did.

It very quickly became apparent that the weather was very poor. I nevertheless continued and became increasingly preoccupied with looking out for electricity pylons and cables as the cloud level and visibility lowered. I reduced speed to about 360 knots and dropped half flap to improve my manœuvrability, and I maintained my heading for the IP, coming fairly close to it. I turned on to the heading for the target. I knew that I had two railway lines at right angles to my track and that there was some eight to nine miles between them; thus if the weather was still bad after I had passed the first railway line, I could still turn port on to an easterly heading confident that there was no high ground before the second railway line. Unfortunately, in my preoccupation with the weather I had not restarted my stopwatch at the IP and was thus, in terms of my navigation, situationally very unaware. I had allowed my determination to succeed to override common sense and good airmanship and also to disregard the ASIs. I was an accident waiting to happen. The wait was quite short.

Seeing a railway track pass underneath me and with the weather very quickly becoming much worse, I decided to turn on to the easterly heading and so avoid the higher ground which I knew was 'down track' beyond the second railway line. Most regrettably, the railway track I saw, although I didn't know it, was the second track, and so as I turned on to the easterly heading I was unwittingly flying towards increasingly higher ground. I added to my already very poor decisions: I did not carry out an emergency bad-weather abort, which required full power and a steep angle of climb that would almost certainly, given the area over which I was flying, risk infringing the lower levels of civilian-controlled airspace. Instead I decided to climb at a shallow angle on the easterly heading, which I knew would take me into better weather below the controlled airspace

Above and below: Damage to Swift 'E' (WK278) following Flight Lieutenant (as he then was) Pat King's unintended encounter with some of the arboreal features of the West German landscape.

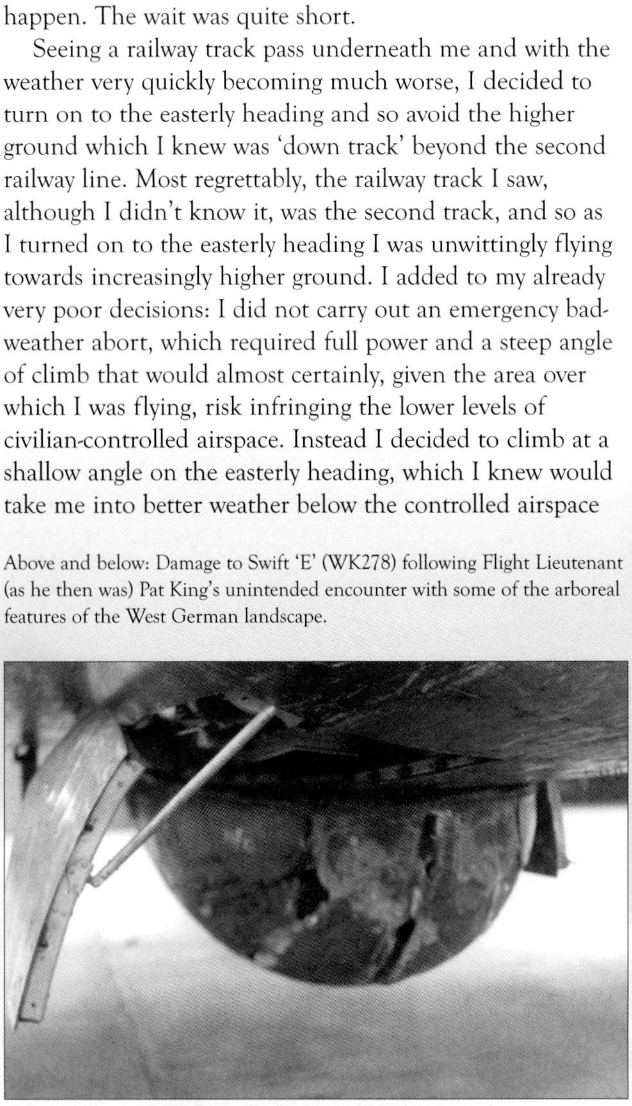

COURTESY PAT KING

and so allow me to drop down to low level en route to the second target.

By this time I was in cloud and in a shallow climb. Although I cannot be certain of the time, I estimate that within 20 to 30 seconds, instead of the grey cloud I was seeing, it all turned green. I remembered 'in a flash', from my conversion to the single-seat Swift (there were no dual Swifts), the advice of Bunny Warren, our Squadron A1 QFI, who said that, as the Swift was a pretty heavy flying object, if you ever over-rotated you would get a 'high speed stall' and continue the same flight path until you recovered. He also said that a high-speed stall in a Swift would occur much sooner than you would expect if you were flying a Hunter (which I had been flying before joining the Squadron). In these circumstances I had no height for a recovery!

His advice notwithstanding, I pulled pretty rapidly back on the stick. Seemingly instantaneously, there was a horrible banging and I saw the ventral belly tank 'doll's eye' go white (which meant that the tank was punctured), the engine rpm unwind and the jet pipe temperature (jpt) increase. As I was by now climbing at a reasonable angle, I took a quick look to ensure that the ejection seat pin was in its correct position. It was. I swapped hands on the stick and flew the aircraft with my left hand, my right hand grasping the ejection-seat handle above my head. I simply held the wings level while monitoring the rpm and jpt. After what seemed an age (but probably wasn't), both the rpm and the jpt stabilised. In the interim, I did not attempt to do anything to the engine on the basis of that simple adage, 'If it's working, don't fix it'. I continued my IFR climb, popping out on top at about 6,000–7,000 feet.

I headed for Gütersloh and made a pan call on the approach frequency, receiving no response; I later found out that I had left all the underside aerials in a pine forest. When I was almost in the overhead I again made a call and this time received a reply. I explained that I thought I had hit some trees. I repeated my statement, which was acknowledged, and asked if any aircraft returning to base would give me an airborne check. A Hunter friend came to my aid and flew on my starboard wing, underneath, and then to my port wing. What he had to say was not particularly encouraging. I carried out a low-speed handling check to ensure that I had adequate control on the final approach, and set up for a 'flame out' landing in case the engine failed completely as I reduced power. In the event, the landing went okay.

Towards the end of the roll-out, I saw my fans in the form of the Station Commander, the Wing Commander Flying, assorted others and some Squadron mates. The last waved encouragingly at me with Winston Churchill victory salutes, and I thought how nice it was of them to show support in what I knew was shortly to be my hour of need.

I won't comment on the Board of Inquiry, or much else, except to say that my situation was not helped by both the aircraft and engine being written off and that the tree felling had occurred outside an authorised low-flying area. In due course, the Air Officer Commanding RAF Germany invited me down to see him and was kind enough to give me some clear career advice.

Although others might disagree, I am convinced to this day that if I had been flying a Hunter I would not have survived, because, while the Hunter was a delight to fly, Supermarine built super-solid aircraft. Thank goodness!

Fun to Fly *Group Captain John Turner*

The Swift, having failed in the contest with the Hunter to be the next air-to-air fighter, reappeared in its modified form as a tactical reconnaissance aircraft—the F.R.5. This was the only version of the aircraft that I flew as a member of No 79 Squadron, based in Germany. There were no two-seat versions, so the conversion procedure was simple: (1) check out in the Hunter; (2) read the Swift Pilot's Notes; (3) go!

The evaluators were right: the Swift's performance at high level left a good deal to be desired, and, quite rightly, the Hunter gained the crown. However, in its new guise, and in its new rôle at low level, it was a very different kettle of fish, offering a remarkably stable platform at 540 knots at very low level and able to match any other comparable aircraft at that time. The Swift picked up a poor reputation as a result of its competition with the Hunter which remained with it for most of its life, but this was not justified in its new rôle.

The aircraft was a pleasure to fly at low level, and the low-flying areas of Germany provided an excellent training ground. It was the only aircraft I have ever flown 'hands off' while swapping target maps from the left- to right-hand pockets when flying at such heights and speeds. Such was its stability. We managed to prove the point when Sandy Cobban and I won the team award at the International Reconnaissance Competition, 'Royal Flush'.

Not that the aircraft was without its faults. While it was very forgiving in all low-level manœuvres, the engine did have a habit of stopping, particularly during medium- to high-level activities. Moreover, it did need every ounce of power to get airborne, which meant applying full hydraulic brakes at the take-off point, and letting the aircraft 'soak' in full reheat until the required jet-pipe temperature was reached, whereupon the brakes were released. It used to amuse me, when taking off from West Raynham, to reach the top of the hump in the runway and to see the Safeland barrier being lowered at the other end—clearly indicating the Controller's fear that I might not quite get airborne in time.

Sadly, engine failure happened all too often, leading to many ejections (my own among them). Indeed, these reached the point that it was suggested, in jest, that operational ties not be awarded until one had jumped out! Having said that, my lasting impression of the Swift is one of great affection. The aircraft was fun to fly, and it was excellent in its operational rôle of tactical reconnaissance.

TESTING FOR THE FUTURE

Group Captain Nigel Walpole OBE BA

NOTWITHSTANDING the failure of the early Swifts as air defence fighters, there remained some residual hope that further developments in the aircraft could return it to that rôle. Evidence of this is recorded in Contract No 9757, which called for the production of 75 Swift F. Mk 7s, equipped to carry the Fireflash first-generation air-to-air missile and its successor Firestreak. These hopes were dashed when the contract was cancelled, but it was replaced by No 9929, for two prototypes and ten F.7s, to carry out trials with the Fireflash.

The F.7 was based on the concept of a high-flying photo-reconnaissance Swift P.R.6, of which one example was built but never flew. The nose of this aircraft had been extended to accommodate the cameras, and this space was now to be occupied by the radar-ranging equipment for the Fireflash. The guns were removed to reduce the aircraft's overall weight, while the wingspan was increased and a more powerful Avon 116 engine (with reheat) fitted to improve performance at high level.

Fireflash originated in 1949 as 'Blue Sky', a beam-riding AAM developed by Fairy Aviation of Heston, to the Ministry's OR.1080, against the perceived threat from Soviet 'Bull' (B-29 copy) piston-engine bombers, flying at heights around 35,000 feet. The pilot of the launch aircraft was required to maintain a radar beam on the target until the Mach 2 missile impacted or its proximity fuse was triggered in a near-miss. As such, the missile could be effective only against aircraft with limited manœuvrability, not against fighters in combat.

To get the programme under way as soon as possible, pending delivery of two F.7 prototypes and the production models a Swift F.4 (WK279) was modified to accept two Fireflash for missile carriage trials. This was followed in 1956 by live missile firings from the two prototypes (XF774 and XF778) on the ranges in Cardigan Bay, the aircraft flying from the Guided Weapons Development Squadron (GWDS), stationed at RAF Valley and commanded by Wing Commander Joe Dalley.

Opinions on the aircraft itself varied. Joe, the most experienced of the trials pilots, recalls that the F.7 was pleasant to fly and, importantly, 'rock steady' as a weapons platform. Others thought differently. With comments not unlike those voiced by pilots on the F.1 and F.2; they claimed that, at height, the aircraft was only really happy flying in a straight line, that it was otherwise heavy and cumbersome, and that it was 'generally disliked' by most. Trial reports showed considerable variation in the abilities of the GWDS pilots to track a steady target accurately, with the central dot in the optical sight remaining within the 0.25 degrees required, up to a height of 45,000 feet, particularly when the auto-stabilisers in the aircraft were inoperative, but, again, Joe Dalley had few difficulties—even with the 'autostabs' off.

COURTESY PHILIP JARRETT

Above: XF124, the last of fourteen Swift Mk 7s to have been completed. These aircraft were based on the ill-fated Mk 6 photo-reconnaissance Swift, and were equipped to carry Fireflash beam-riding air-to-air missiles—designed to home in on their target so long as the Swift pilot continued to track the target accurately. The extended wing tips of this mark are evident here. Below: A Fireflash missile is sent on its way in a trial firing. In genuine combat, the inability of the Swift pilot to manœuvre his aircraft as he might wish during the firing phase could have rendered him very vulnerable to enemy attack.

In January 1958 an interim report was submitted on the F.7's performance as a launch aircraft for Fireflash, but live firings continued until November 1958 and a final report, which analysed the findings, was not issued until mid-1959. It concluded that a success rate of 86 per cent could be achieved in attacks made from directly astern of large targets, flying straight and level at 35,000 feet, but that this rate would drop off markedly if the target was higher

COURTESY PHILIP JARRETT

COURTESY PHILIP JARRETT

or took evasive action, if the attack was made from anything but directly astern, or if the autostabs were inoperative. Even with these reservations, GWDS pilots considered this claim to be over-optimistic: they questioned the efficacy of the proximity fuse, were greatly concerned that the fighter would not be able to manœuvre in hostile airspace during the tracking phase, and considered that the system would probably be ineffective at heights below 8,000 feet because of radar attenuation with the ground.

The GWDS pilots had ample grounds for such opinions on the F.7/Fireflash combination, with the unit having flown 2,400 hours on the aircraft in some twenty months, happily with fewer defects or incidents in the air than had been the case in the sad saga of the Swift's introduction with the F.1 and F.2.

In fact, only three incidents were recorded. In the first, an explosive bolt fired by accident, allowing a missile to fall harmlessly on to the concrete below. The resulting modification underlined the value of the trials—preventing any recurrence of the fault. Shortly thereafter, a panel on the nose of the aircraft, which protected the radar-ranging and had not been fastened securely before flight, became detached in the air, giving the pilot the erroneous impression that he had engine problems. This was an incident waiting to happen, with the Swift's many screw

COURTESY PHILIP JARRETT

AD HOC COLLECTION

Opposite page and below: Publicity photographs showing Fireflash missiles being mounted and adjusted on the carrier aircraft. The weapon weighed some 330 pounds and had an overall length of 9 feet 6 inches. It was powered by two external rocket motors, giving it a boosted speed of approximately Mach 2, but their fuel was expended very quickly, leaving the missile to continue to its target under it own momentum, at a rapidly reducing speed. Its maximum range was about two miles. Above: Another of the Swift F.7s, XF119, with a pair of Fireflashes. The missile was tested extensively, but it was superseded by the much more effective 'fire and forget' De Havilland Firestreak infra-red homing AAM.

COURTESY PHILIP JARRETT

COURTESY RICHARD L. WARD

lock fasteners inviting human error, but thereafter all the screw slots had to be aligned with yellow markers before the aircraft was signed off for flight. In the third incident, suspected engine trouble led the pilot to make a hasty landing, at rather too high a speed, which resulted in him running into the overshoot. Joe Dalley also had the frightening experience of a Fireflash booster rocket, with life still in it when it jettisoned from the missile, flying back over his cockpit, but thankfully no harm was done.

If there had been any residual hope that this Swift/Fireflash combination could be developed for operational use it had now gone, but the evaluation had been very well worth while on several counts. A great deal of data had been gleaned on missile handling, procedures in the air and on the ground, performance and storage. Moreover, the ground equipment used in the trials had been tested thoroughly and modified where necessary, servicing procedures had been developed and there had been much 'hands-on' training. Within its known limitations, the Fireflash missile had performed satisfactorily. Its accuracy was as predicted and its reliability acceptable—although it showed worrying signs of rapid deterioration with time and in less than perfect storage conditions.

Diverse comment on the aircraft/weapon combination came thick and fast in the wake of the trials, ranging from very good to very poor. The March 1977 edition of *Aeroplane Monthly* carried a

Left, upper: One of the Swift F.7s, XF114, instead of being employed in missile work, was utilised for, amongst other tasks, exploring the hazards of fast-jet handling on wet runway surfaces. It is seen here at Filton during a trial of this nature. Left, lower, and right: Originally completed in standard RAF camouflage, XF114 was later painted black overall and featured an amusing 'Donald Duck' cartoon on its nose. Below: Later still, distinctive calibration markings were added. For a period, Heathrow Airport was used as a venue for the runway trials.

COURTESY RICHARD L. WARD

quotation, allegedly from a Supermarine engineer, that in his opinion 'the Swift F.7 was the finest and most effective aircraft/weapons combination available to the RAF at that time', and deplored the fact that it had been 'thrown on the scrap-heap . . . just as all the problems had been overcome'. This would surely have been challenged by many of the pilots who had evaluated the system on GWDS and who might have found a later, highly critical view in *Air International* more in keeping with their findings. This suggested, *inter alia*, that a (hypothetical) F.7 pilot could have had great difficulty tracking a current, high-flying, tail-armed bomber—which could hardly be expected to remain straight and level as in idealised trial conditions—with sufficient precision to secure a 'kill' with this system. Drawing on his experience flying Canberra and Valiant bombers, Joe Dalley thought otherwise: his view was that, in the hands of a capable F.7 pilot, this supersonic missile, with its 7–10-second flight time, had the potential to threaten both these types. However, he did not think that the system could have been developed into a viable operational option in the time frame in which it would have been needed. He did claim, with justification, that the GWDS had shown the way ahead for AAMs in demonstrating the limitations of first-generation beam-riding AAMs, and that much of that learned during the trials would help developments in the field. Although intended, the Swift did not get to carry the Firestreak with its infra-red (IR) acquisition head. This missile did not need a radar beam on which to ride nor, therefore, precise tracking by the pilot—it relied solely on a heat source for guidance—but its development into a fully operational weapon benefited much from the Fireflash trials.

This, then, was the end of the Swift story—a very mixed story of failure and success, of exploration, of innovation and of determination. It epitomised the spirit within the aviation industry in the 1950s.

COURTESY RICHARD L. WARD

SQUADRONS AND COLOURS

IN stark contrast to what was originally its direct rival the Hawker Hunter—which was destined to enjoy a stellar career in the Royal Air Force, equipping as it did more than thirty front-line squadrons—the Swift saw very limited service. As we have seen, only one squadron, No 56 (F) at Waterbeach, took delivery of the fighter version, and, the skills of its personnel both aircrew and groundcrew notwithstanding, it was shown to be simply not up to the job for which it was intended. The redesigned F.R.5 was more successful, and indeed proved to be a very useful aircraft, but even so this variant saw service in merely two (or, to stretch technicalities, three) squadrons. The units with which the aircraft served are summarised in the accompanying table.

In terms of colours, the Swift F.1 was only ever finished in overall High Speed Silver. Subsequent marks in service—F.2, F.R.5 and F.7—had their upper surfaces sprayed in a disruptive camouflage pattern of glossy Dark Sea Grey and Dark Green. The undersides of the F.2 and F.7 were silver, but, in keeping with the photo-reconnaissance rôle, F.R.5s generally had PRU Blue undersurfaces although silver-bellied Mk 5s were frequently to be seen during the aircraft's latter years of service as the use of PRU Blue was phased out.

FRONT-LINE SWIFT SQUADRONS

Unit	Principal location(s)	Equipment	Remarks
No II (AC) Squadron	Geilenkirchen, Jever	F.R.5s (23/02/56–13/04/61)	Fighter-reconnaissance rôle.
No IV Squadron	Jever	F.R.5s (01/01/61–00/03/61)	Re-formed 01/01/61 out of No 79 Sqn (q.v.). Some Swifts retained until re-equipment with Hunters completed.
No 56 (F) Squadron	Waterbeach	F.1s (20/02/54–15/03/55), F.2s (00/08/54–15/03/55)	Only squadron to fly original interceptor variant.
No 79 Squadron	Wunstorf, Gütersloh,	F.R.5s (14/06/56–30/12/60)	Fighter-reconnaissance rôle.

OTHER SWIFT UNITS

Unit	Principal location(s)	Equipment	Remarks
Aeroplane & Armament Experimental Establishment	Boscombe Down	Prototypes and various marks throughout development period.	Tests and trials.
Royal Aircraft Establishment	Farnborough, Bedford	Various marks.	Tests and trials.
Empire Test Pilots' School	Farnborough	F.7 XF113.	Test-flying.
Air Fighting Development Squadron	West Raynham	Various F.1s and F.R.5s	Component of Central Fighter Establishment.
No 1 Guided Weapons Development Squadron	Valley	F.7s.	Trials and testing.

AUTHOR'S COLLECTION

Above: Officer aircrew of No II (AC) Squadron in a formal photograph taken at RAF Jever in the summer of 1959: (front row, left to right) Flight Lieutenants Bob Barcilon, 'Bunny' St Aubyn and Eric Sharp, Squadron Leader Chris Wade (CO), and Flight Lieutenants Benji Hives, Roy Rimington and Maurice Dale; (back row, left to right) Flight Lieutenants Peter Adair, Bill Sheppard, Ben Gunn, Phil Crawshaw, Danny Brooks, Phil Hoden-Rushworth, George Hagan and 'Taff' Wallis.
Below: Officers of No 79 Squadron at Gütersloh in 1958: (front row, left to right) Flying Officer Pete Farris, Flight Lieutenants Sandy Cobham, Pete Terry and John Gale, Squadron Leader Hugh Harrison (CO), and Flight Lieutenants Geoffrey Lee, Brian Seaman, Mick Davis and Roger Pyrah; (back row, left to right) Flying Officer Roy Chitty, Flight Lieutenant Glyn Chapman, Flying Officer 'Kiwi' Graves, and Flight Lieutenants Derek Meeks, John Turner, Nigel Walpole, Nick Carter, 'Fergie' Ferguson and 'Harv' Harvie.

AUTHOR'S COLLECTION

COURTESY TONY BUTTLER

COURTESY TONY BUTTLER

Top: Swift F. 1 WK205 on charge to the Air Fighting Development Squadron at West Raynham, finished in the High Speed Silver scheme which also characterised this particular mark in service with No 56 (F) Squadron at Waterbeach.
Above: A photograph taken at RAF Gütersloh, with WK310 central in the frame and displaying a red outline to its squadron markings.
Below: Flight Lieutenant (now Squadron Leader) Roy Rimington attending the Battle of Britain Display at RAF Biggin Hill on 17 September 1960, his mount for the day, Swift F.R.5 XD962/'J' (the aircraft the CO normally flew—note the Squadron Leader's pennant on the nose), in the background.
Right: F.R.5 WK303 of No 79 Squadron photographed at *circa* 25,000 feet and hurtling earthwards. Whilst the Swift's underwing serials were always very prominently displayed, the fuselage serials, tucked beneath the tailplane, were less easily seen—especially on the port side where a Dark Green camouflage band intruded. For this reason, many FR Swifts had their fuselage serials painted in white.

COURTESY ROY RIMINGTON

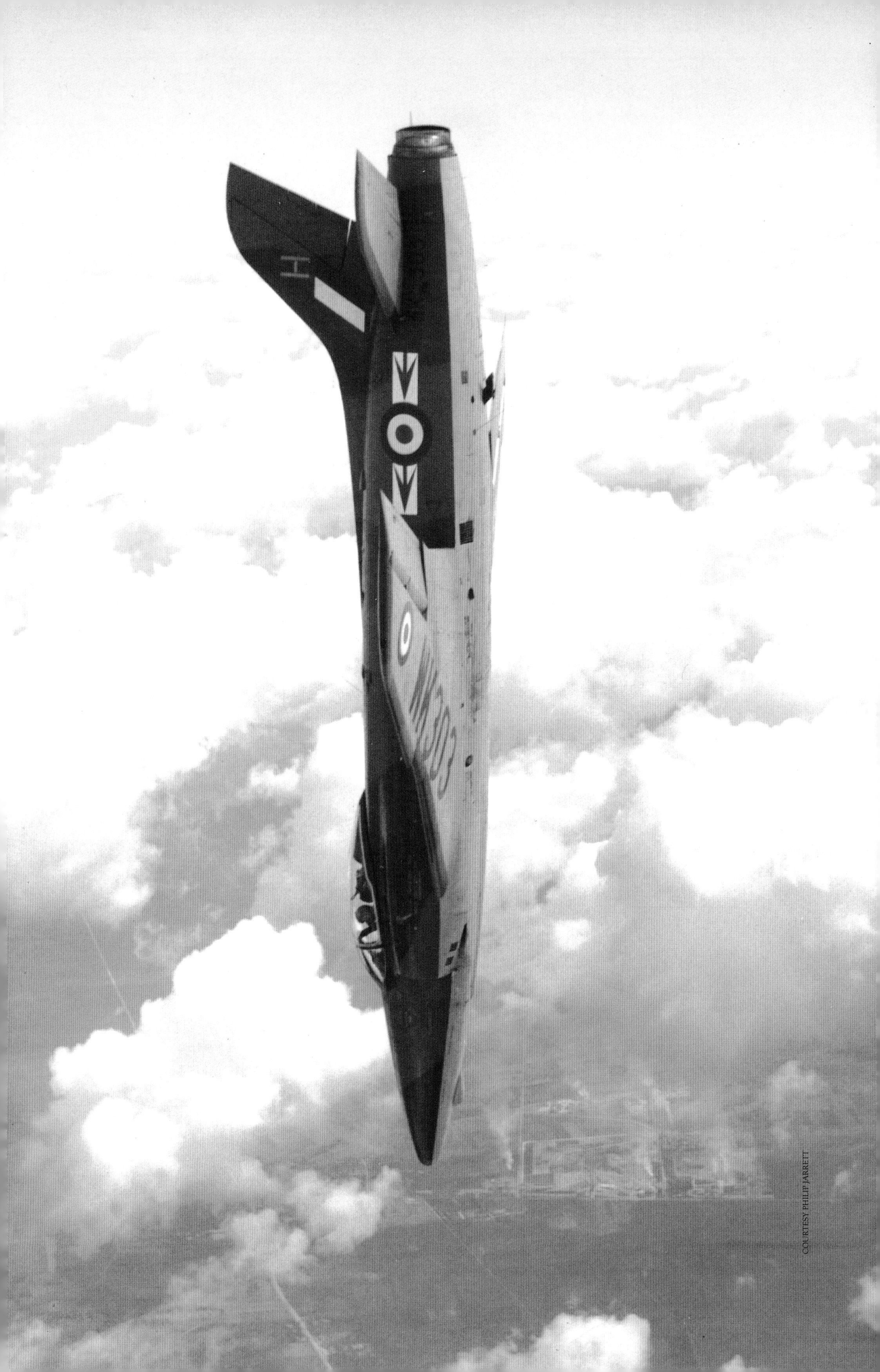

COURTESY PHILIP JARRETT

Supermarine Swift F. Mk 4 WK198, World Air Speed Record holder,
Idris Airfield, Libya, September 1953

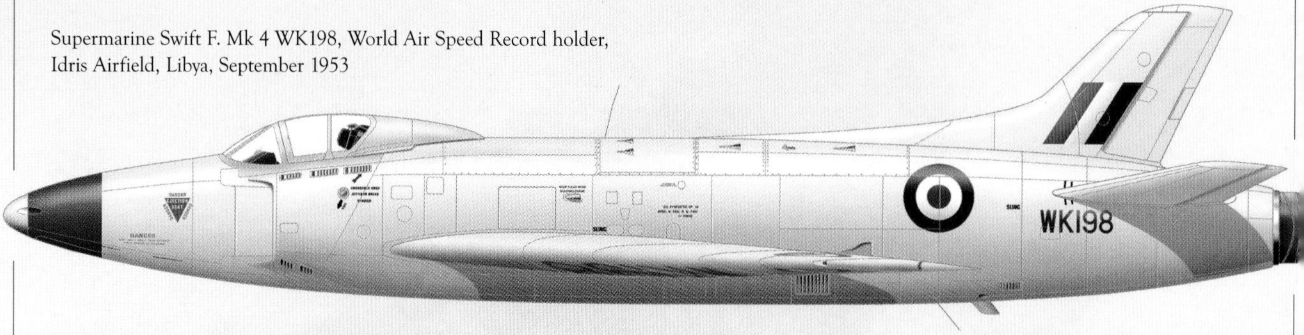

Supermarine Swift F. Mk 1 WK209, No 56 (F) Squadron (first delivery),
RAF Waterbeach, March 1954

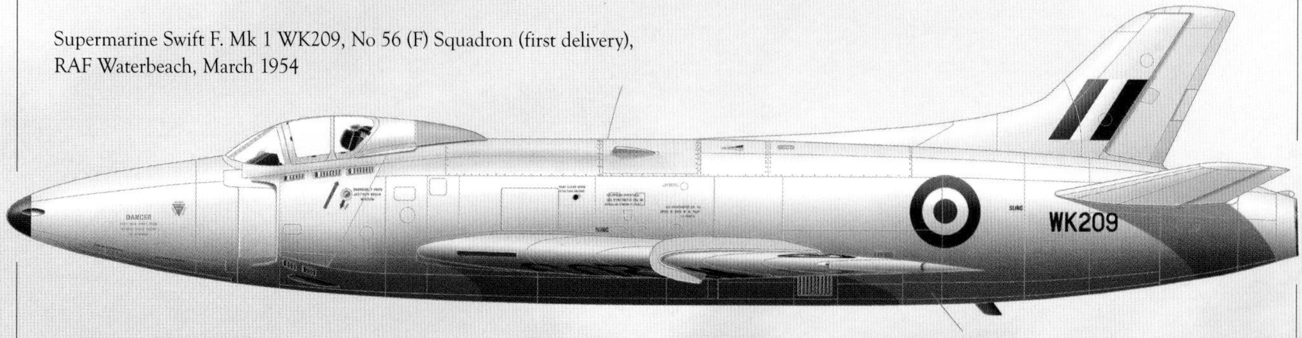

Supermarine Swift F. Mk 1 WK205, Air Fighting Development Squadron,
RAF West Raynham, April 1954

Supermarine Swift F. Mk 1 WK207, No 56 (F) Squadron,
RAF Waterbeach, May 1954

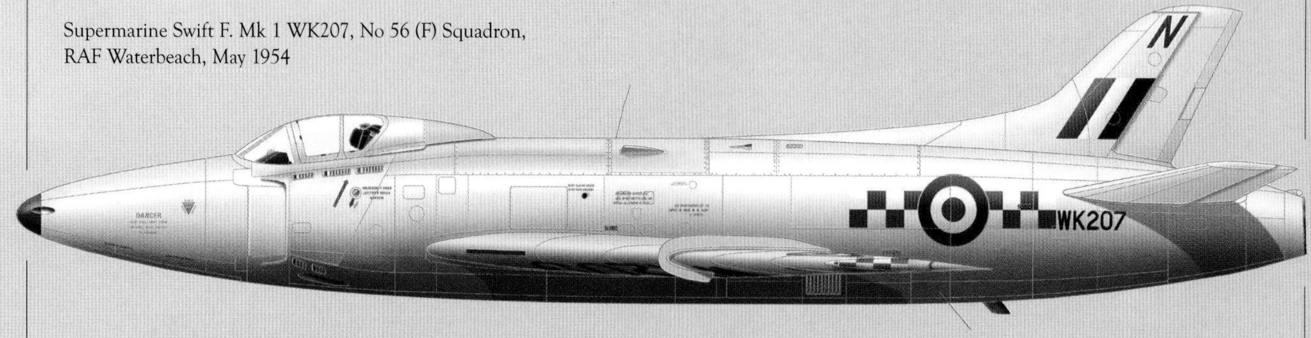

Supermarine Swift F. Mk 2 WK245, No 56 (F) Squadron,
RAF Waterbeach, November 1954

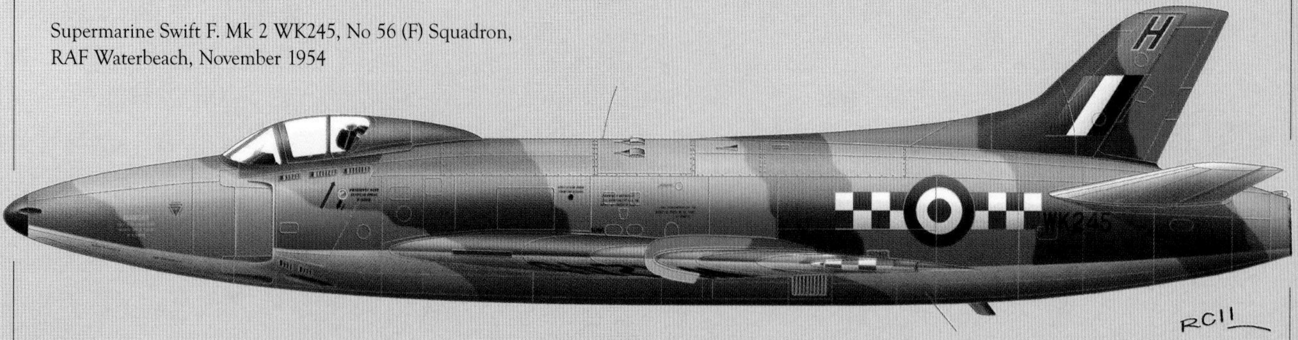

Supermarine Swift F.R. Mk 5 XD925, No 79 Squadron (first delivery), RAF Wunstorf, June 1956

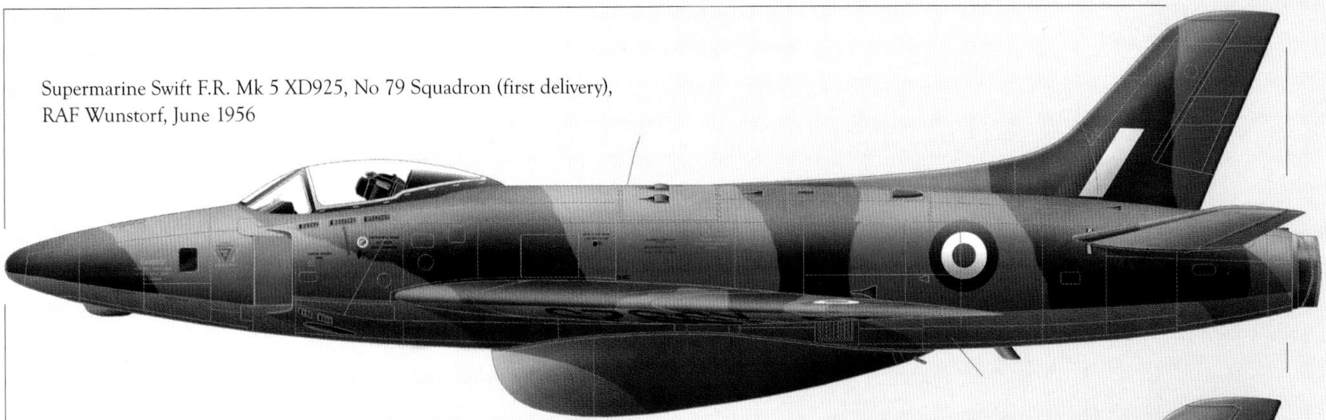

Supermarine Swift F. Mk 7 XF116, No 1 Guided Weapons Development Squadron, RAF Valley , November 1957

Supermarine Swift F.R. Mk 5 XD930, No II (AC) Squadron, RAF Jever, December 1959

Supermarine Swift F.R. Mk 5 XD962, No II (AC) Squadron, RAF Jever, September 1960

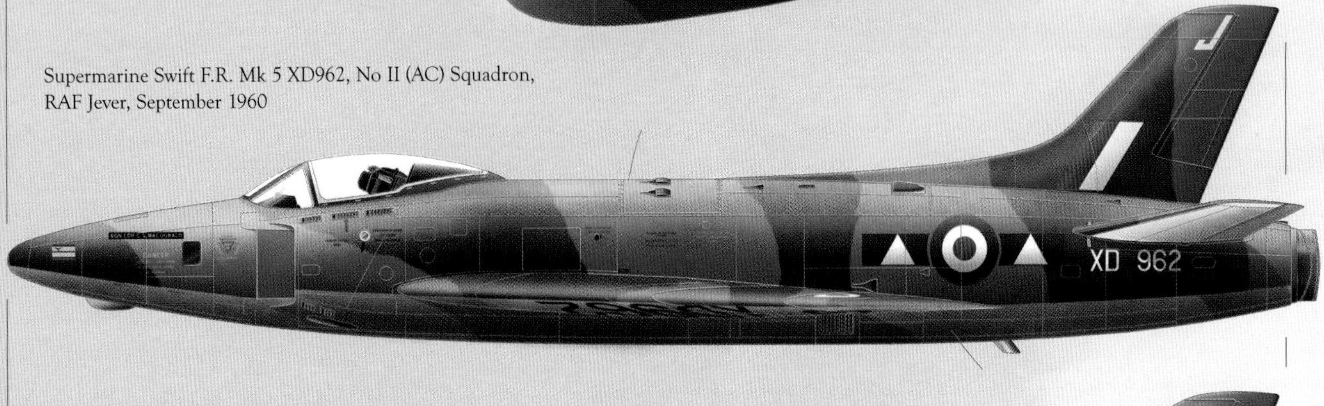

Supermarine Swift F.R. Mk 5 WK293, No IV Squadron, RAF Gütersloh, summer 1961

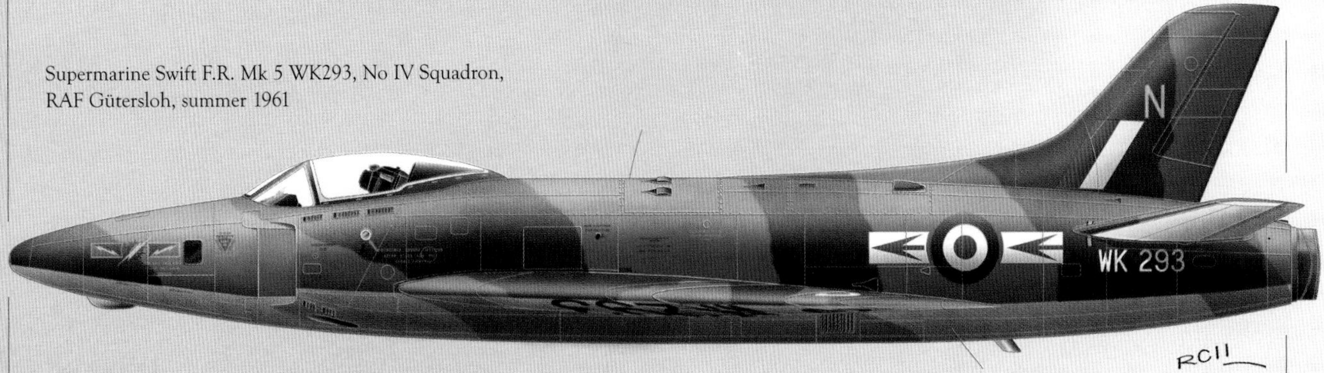

FLOWN BY THE AUTHOR

SUPERMARINE SWIFT F. R. Mk 5
WK281, No 79 Squadron, RAF Gütersloh, April 1959

GONE BUT NOT FORGOTTEN

Group Captain Nigel Walpole OBE BA

VERY few Swift airframes remain to help us remember that remarkable period of innovation and enterprise in the 1950s, which were formative years for a new generation of jet fighters. The experimental Supermarine Type 510, which helped pioneer swept-wing flight, has survived, seemingly unwanted in RAF heritage but welcomed by the Royal Navy at the Fleet Air Arm Museum, Yeovilton. Its sister aircraft, which achieved fame as 'Prometheus' in David Lean's film *The Sound Barrier*, was not so lucky: its ultimate fate is unknown. Other early models ended up as instructional airframes, in trials on nuclear effects held at Maralinga, Australia, or in scrapyards throughout Britain.

This might have been a final resting place for the most famous Swift of all, WK198, originally an F.1 but modified to become the F.4 prototype, the aircraft in which Mike Lithgow wrested the World Air Speed Record from the Americans on 25 September1953. Fortunately, just as its last rites were about to be read at the Unimetals scrapyard in Failsworth, Oldham, it was rescued and taken to the North East Aircraft Museum in Sunderland. There, every attempt was made to find wings and other major parts for the aircraft, but with no success, and at the time of writing, it is believed that only the fuselage shell and tailplane remain to be seen.

Another F.4 (WK275), featuring the slab tail and sawtooth leading edges to the wings, resides outside Sheppards Store at Upper Hill, Leominster. Exposed to the elements, it continues to deteriorate, and there is no question of it flying again.

At one time, there was some hope that F.7 XF114 would be brought up to flying status. It had a chequered career, beginning life as a trials aircraft, before its use as a fast-jet familiarisation aircraft for pilots destined for the Supermarine Scimitar and later for wet-runway braking trials. It was struck off charge in 1967. The all but complete aircraft then went to the North East Wales Institute of Higher Education, at Connah's Quay, as an instructional airframe. At that time the engine could be run and some of its basic systems were operative, suggesting that XF114 might indeed fly again. Protracted negotiations led finally, in 1989, to the aircraft's acquisition by Jet Heritage at Hurn Airport, Bournemouth, where enthusiasts were determined to bring it back to life. Sadly it was not to be: various factors combined to cause the demise of Jet Heritage, and the release of XF114 to a private owner. At the time of writing, the aircraft's whereabouts are not known, and it would seem that all chances of getting it airborne again have now gone.

Below and opposite page: Unwanted and unloved, and stripped of anything of worth, redundant Swift F.R.5s, late of No II Squadron, rot in scrapyards. The Swift interceptor was quickly replaced in service by the Hunter; the fighter-reconnaissance version fended off its rival for a few years but in the end it, too, succumbed to the same fate. CO Squadron Leader MacDonald's pennant can still be made out on the nose of XD962 (opposite, top).

COURTESY RICHARD L. WARD

COURTESY RICHARD L. WARD

Two airframes remain in good condition, a No II Squadron F.R.5 (WK277) at Newark Air Museum and a No 79 Squadron F.R.5 (WK281) at Tangmere Military Aviation Museum. WK277 originated as an F.4, and as such flew first from Supermarine's factory at South Marston in 1955. It was converted to an F.R.5 in 1956 and, after a lengthy period in storage, arrived at RAF Jever in March 1959. In its two years of service there it suffered major damage on two occasions, but was repaired and returned to Britain when the F.R.5s were withdrawn from service, to become an instructional airframe at RAF Cosford. When declared redundant, WK277 was purchased by Vickers Armstrong test pilot 'Dizzy' Addicott, who intended to convert it into a jet car for an attempt on the land speed record. When this project was shelved, the aircraft was bought by Norman Pratlett, and displayed at Newark, where it remains to this day.

WK281 was delivered to the RAF in 1956, but it, too, did not reach the front line until 1959, where it served on No 79 Squadron, as the author's personal aircraft, 'Sierra', without major incident until its retirement in 1961. The aircraft was then flown to No 60 MU at RAF Church Fenton, and thereafter went by road to the Air Training Corps squadron at Uxbridge. In 1967, 'Sierra' was given a shiny new camouflage finish, to be displayed first at an RAF

COURTESY PHILIP JARRETT

Right: Swift F.R.5 WK277, which saw service with No II Squadron, is preserved and accessible to the public at the Newark Air Museum in Lincolnshire.
Below: A second F.R.5, WK281, is housed at the Tangmere Military Aviation Museum in Sussex; coincidentally, this is the aircraft that the author regularly flew when he served on No 79 Squadron.

AUTHOR

Abingdon Air Show, then at the RAF Museum, Hendon, and now at Tangmere, where staff have carried out considerable refurbishment.

It is now most unlikely that any Swift will take to the air ever again, but it would be a travesty to forget the aircraft or recall it solely as a failure as so many have done. True, it should not have remained on the front line in the fighter rôle, but by the time it was withdrawn from that rôle all the early variants had been invaluable in exploring new technology for transonic/supersonic flight, typically in swept-wing forms, flying tails and reheat. Moreover, the F.R.5 proved to be an ideal platform for armed reconnaissance, given its stability at very low level and unprecedented high speeds. It proved itself in TACEVALS, national and international reconnaissance competitions and was well liked by most of its pilots. Contrary to much loose talk, the aircraft was not a 'killer', although it certainly had its technical defects, many of which had to be attributed to the engine; as remarked earlier, only one pilot was killed in an F.R.5 on the front line, and that was as a result of a servicing error. Nor should the contribution made by the F.7 be overlooked, as it explored every aspect of the new science surrounding the beam-riding air-to-air-missile. Supermarine did not achieve what it had hoped for with the Swift, but it deserves great credit for its enterprise, innovation, industry and determination—and for what it added to the era of second-generation jet fighters.

AUTHOR